MW00476619

The Night Has a Naked Soul

The Night Has a Naked Soul

Witchcraft and Sorcery among the Western Cherokee

Alan Kilpatrick

SYRACUSE UNIVERSITY PRESS

Copyright © 1997 by Syracuse University Press
Syracuse, New York 13244-5160
All Rights Reserved

First Paperback Edition 1998
98 99 00 01 02 03   6 5 4 3 2 1

The paper used in this publication meets the minimum requirements of
American National Standard for Information Sciences—Permanence of Paper
for Printed Library Materials, ANSI Z39.48-1984. ∞™

Library of Congress Cataloging-in-Publication Data

Kilpatrick, Alan.
The night has a naked soul : witchcraft and sorcery among the
western Cherokee / Alan Kirkpatrick. — 1st ed.
p.   cm.
Includes bibliographical references and index.
ISBN 0-8156-0471-8 (cloth : alk. paper) ISBN 0-8156-0539-0 (pbk.: alk. paper)
1. Cherokee Indians—Rites and ceremonies.   2. Cherokee
incantations.   3. Cherokee magic.   4. Shamanism—Oklahoma.
5. Witchcraft—Oklahoma.   I. Title.
E99.C5K45   1997
299'.7855—dc21   97-12690

Manufactured in the United States of America

In Memoriam:
Tse:gi and E:ne

Alan Kilpatrick is associate professor of American Indian studies at San Diego State University. His articles on Cherokee religion have appeared in *American Indian Quarterly* and in *American Indian Culture and Research Journal*.

Contents

Numbered Texts

Preface

My ambitions for this book could not have been realized without an extraordinary amount of help from institutions and individuals as well. First, I am grateful to the College of Arts and Letters at San Diego State University, which funded the initial fieldwork.

I was also fortunate to receive institutional support from the Bienecke Rare Book and Manuscript Library at Yale University where I was allowed as an Archibald Hanna, Jr., Visiting Fellow to spend a blustery but productive winter in New Haven. I thank Mr. George Miles, curator of the Western Americana collection at the Bienecke, who kindly permitted me to reproduce the majority of the Cherokee texts that are presented between these covers.

The manuscript was reviewed by Lawrence Hauptman, editor of the Syracuse University Iroquois series, and by Floyd Lounsbury, professor emeritus of anthropology, Yale University. I am grateful to both individuals for their criticisms. I am also indebted to Sergei Kan and John Watanabe of Dartmouth College who, upon reading an earlier version of this work, suggested that I make the book more "anthropological." I hope that I have met their expectations.

Among Cherokee scholars I thank Janine Scancarelli, William and Mary College, who has been particularly generous in sharing her time and expertise with me. Another continual source of inspiration and encouragement to me has been Raymond Fogelson of the University of Chicago.

To my coterie of Cherokee informants I express my heartfelt thanks. I particularly thank Levi and Virginia Carey whose Cherokee linguistic skills were instrumental in bringing this research to completion. In addition, I received invaluable insights into the Cherokee world of the occult from a number of my relatives who prefer to remain anonymous. I was also fortunate to have the services of Bardy Anderson, whose skillful hands drew the maps.

Finally, an irreplaceable source of love and support over the last few years has been my wife, Joan. So to her and our two "girls," Phoebe and Penguina, this book is affectionately dedicated.

San Diego, California
September 1996

Alan Kilpatrick

Introduction

Human beings seem to have an incurable fascination with magic and supernaturalism. Judging from the range of occult activities recorded on Paleolithic rock carvings in Europe (Gimbutas 1989), on papyri from ancient Egypt (Wilson 1951, 243; Griffith 1904–9), and in the oral traditions of Tungus-speaking peoples of Siberia (Eliade 1964), the belief that individuals can engender through formulated spells and curses alchemistic transformations of their environment has continued unabated throughout the centuries.

The phenomenon of witchcraft and sorcery also appears to be a universal constant in human societies. Some of the earliest ruminations on the subject of maleficence come from medieval Europe. Perhaps the most notable example of this early scholarship is the work of James the First who, inspired by the diabolical inquisitions of the *zauberwahn*, published his tract, *Daemonologie*, in 1597. It was not until 1890, however, when Sir James Frazer published his monumental tome, *The Golden Bough*, that magic in all its forms received a comprehensive intellectual treatment.

Some of the earliest and most vivid reportage on native superstitions in the Americas comes from sixteenth-century Franciscan missionaries Fray Bernardo Sahagun, *Florentine Codex*, and Fray Diego Duran, *Historia de las Indias de Nueva España e Islas de Tierra Firme*. In addition, Hernando Ruiz de Alarcon's 1629 compilation of seventeenth-century Nahua spells and incantations, *Tratado de las supersticiones de los Naturales de esta Nueva España*, remains a rich source of information on pre-Columbian folk beliefs.

The publication of Evans-Pritchard's classic monograph, *Witchcraft, Oracles, and Magic among the Azande*, in 1937 did much to stimulate modern anthropological interest in the occult. Most of this research has focused on defining the psychosocial ramifications of supernaturalism in nonwestern tribal societies, particularly in Africa (Wilson 1957; Middleton 1963; and Mair 1969).

Native American forms of witchcraft and sorcery have received serious ethnographic treatment only during the twentieth century. The publication of Clyde Kluckhohn's study, *Navajo Witchcraft*, in 1944 began a trend of investigation that continued among southwestern tribes with Keith Basso, *Western Apache Witchcraft*, (1969) and Bahr et al., *Piman Shamanism and Staying Sickness* (1974).

Although there had been sporadic references to the activities of conjurors and witches among the eastern Cherokee during the colonial period (e.g., Adair [1775] 1930), it was not until 1891 that these occult beliefs received serious scholarly attention. During that year the gifted ethnographer James Mooney published his classic work, *The Sacred Formulas of the Cherokee*. Mooney's pioneering research was then revised and expanded upon by his posthumous collaborator, the Belgium linguist Frans Olbrechts, who published *The Swimmer Manuscript* in 1932.

In the 1960s my late parents, Jack Frederick Kilpatrick and Anna Gritts Kilpatrick, both of whom were of Cherokee heritage, began an intellectual odyssey into the medicomagical realm of the Oklahoma Cherokee by interviewing scores of traditional Cherokee folk healers and by acquiring from friends, relatives, and total strangers a vast number of the Cherokee medicine books.

For well over one hundred years the Cherokee Indians have been recording their magical texts in the native script of the Sequoyah syllabary and preserving them in pocket-size ledger notebooks. The Cherokee sacred formulae, which are known as *idi:gawé:sdi* ('to say it, one'), encompass a whole realm of esoteric knowledge relating to such matters as love magic, protective charms, divinatory rituals, and purification rites. In effect these *idi:gawé:sdi* represent the accumulated wisdom of that unique Cherokee institution the medicine man, or *dida:hnvwi:sgi* ('curer of them, he/she').

The Kilpatricks then expended their energies by translating enormous numbers of these magical formulae. The accumulation of their labors resulted in a series of books and monographs whose principal titles include *Friends of Thunder* (1964); *Walk in Your Soul* (1965); *Run Toward the Nightland* (1967); and *Notebook of a Cherokee Shaman* (1970).

After their deaths, this extraordinary collection of Cherokee writings was purchased by the Bienecke Rare Book and Manuscript Library at Yale University where it resides today in the Western Americana section, cataloged as the Uwe:da:sadhi Sa:wali Collection. In retrospect my parents amassed a truly staggering collection of Cherokee manuscripts, which date primarily from the late 1880s to the mid-1960s. In addition to the arcane medicine books, which contain approximately three thousand medicomagical formulae preserved between the covers of some three hundred pocket-size bound notebooks, there are hundreds of loose sheets that relate to the social history of the Oklahoma Cherokee, official correspondence, personal letters, and church records, all of which are written in the Sequoyah syllabary.

Despite the availability of these remarkable, but neglected, native documents, the only modern anthropological studies of Cherokee magical folk beliefs are those undertaken in the 1970s by Raymond Fogelson of the University of Chicago (1971, 1975, 1977, and 1979). In one of his articles Fogelson observed that "Cherokee sorcery and witchcraft beliefs have been studied and restudied for over eighty years by anthropologists. Despite this continous effort, there is still no comprehensive picture of this complex subject" (Fogelson 1975, 114).

It is my hope that this current volume partially fills this void. However, studying the behavior of one's own kin, even in the guise of an anthropologist, strikes me as a singularly myopic task. In many ways it is like observing the movements of one's own shadow.

Despite such misgivings, in 1991 I began the trek down the perilous path of my Cherokee predecessors. Over four years I translated, in part or in full, many of these orphaned Cherokee texts. During this process I began an extensive anthropological investigation of the phenomena of witchcraft and sorcery beliefs among my mother's people. The result is, of course, this volume.

To enhance my analysis I have woven together personal experiences (as a child I knew many of the folk healers whose work is presented here) and insights gleaned from conversations with relatives and informants. I have also used an unpublished corpus of anthropological field notes, magical texts, and personal letters that recently have come into my possession.

The target group of this study is what I term the "western" Cherokee. The main membership of this group can be defined geographically as those individuals who have grown up and now reside in five adjacent counties in northeastern Oklahoma: Sequoyah, Adair, Cherokee, Hayes, and Delaware. Since the nineteenth century, these five counties have comprised the heart of the Cherokee Nation (see map 1).

Although more than 150,000 people proclaim membership in the Cherokee Nation of Oklahoma (a claim that is largely substantiated by blood quantum and federal roll numbers), the group under investigation here, the "traditionalists," comprises only a fraction of that number.

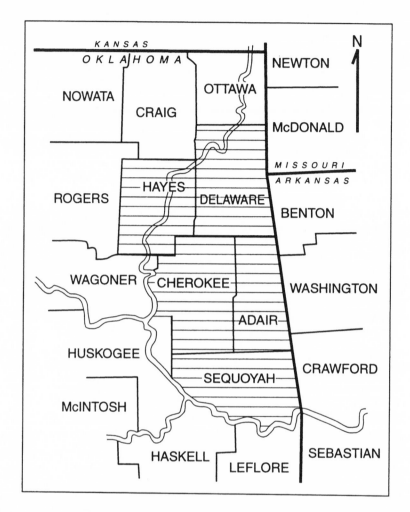

Map 1. Location of the Oklahoma Cherokees

Cherokees whom I deem traditionalist are those persons with a high degree of Indian blood who are known to be conservative members of their communities. To qualify matters further most of these traditionalist Cherokee are still fluent in their native language or are literate in the Sequoyan script. Not surprisingly, the majority of these Cherokees are of my mother's generation, whose inbred beliefs in magic and supernaturalism remain relatively steadfast despite the passage of time.

It should be noted that folk beliefs in witches and sorcerers are not confined to a few rural counties in northeastern Oklahoma. To a lesser extent I include commentary and testimonies from displaced traditionalist Cherokees living as far away as Crawford County, Arkansas; Glendale, California; and Buffalo, New York.

In this essentially "text-bound" monograph I focus on two conceptual areas: folk beliefs and ritualistic language. In chapter 1 I describe the range of Cherokee beliefs about the supernatural by enumerating the known traits and attributes of witches and sorcerers. In chapter 7 I posit from the perspective of anthropological theory an explanation of why such ancient folk beliefs remain viable to Cherokees living in the twentieth century.

Bracketed between the beginning and ending chapters is a discussion on the critical role that transformational language plays in actualizing magic. As a result I devote chapter 3 to describing how Cherokee practitioners utilize a "sacred discourse" to dramatize their ritual performance and to focus their mental energies.

Finally, in chapters 4 through 7 I present my translations of thirty-nine *idi:gawé:sdi* that have been extracted from the Uwe:da:sadhi Sa:wali Collection at Yale. I have arbitrarily assigned these texts to four categories: divinatory prayers, protective charms, serious conjuring spells, and purification rites.

Cherokee *idi:gawé:sdi* are enormously difficult to translate because of the highly specialized vocabulary that Cherokee practitioners of magic employ to empower their spells. To tease out the nuances and subtleties encoded in each of these magical incantations I have resorted to a close line-by-line English transliteration. In my transcription of the Sequoyan syllabary (which consists of eighty-six phonetic symbols) I employ a standardized orthographic system first developed by Floyd Lounsbury, emeritus professor of anthropology at Yale, and my late father. Each transliteration is followed by an accompanying English commentary to explicate the poetic language and symbolic references contained in each text. I also make occasional inferences about the anthropological nature of Cherokee supernaturalism by "contextualizing" the Cherokee experience within the larger framework of other Native American magical traditions.

My coverage of the Cherokee *idi:gawé:sdi* is not exhaustive. Largely for reasons of space, I exclude from my analysis a large body of Cherokee magical expressions: love magic, rain-making spells, hunting and fishing charms, wealth-gaining formulae, and prescriptives that are essentially medicinal in nature.

Despite these limitations the importance of my research is empowered by the fact that the vast majority of ethnographic literature has been written by non-Indians and represents, in many cases, a distorted and secondhand knowledge of native people. It is extremely rare that authentic Native American folk healers record their thoughts, personal history, or worldview in their *own written* language. These translations of the Uwe:da:sadhi manuscripts, therefore, offer a rare glimpse into the aboriginal mind of the Cherokee folk healer and conjuror.

A few months before my father's death in 1967 he wrote this note: "Recently I read in the *Encyclopedia Britannica* that no [N]ative American society north of Mexico had produced a literature: yet during the past five years alone I have collected from attics, barns, caves, and jars buried in the ground some ten thousand poetical texts, many of which would excite the envy of a Hafiz or a Li Tai Po" (Kilpatrick 1967, 85). More than a quarter-century has passed since my father wrote those words.

To date there has been no modern, comprehensive study of Cherokee supernaturalism. As a result, one can neither identify its most salient characteristics nor place this body of esoteric knowledge in the wider context of the growing anthropological literature on indigenous folk beliefs. It is my hope that this book will challenge the conventional wisdom about Native American folk medicine, witchcraft, and sorcery by introducing into the literature a whole new body of shamanistic thought hitherto unavailable in print.

Having said this, I believe that the reader should be forewarned that the magical texts presented here are considered from the vantage point of the Cherokee traditionalist to be "ritually" dead. That is, their powers to heal or harm anyone have expired over time and have now been strictly nullified. Their inherent magic can only be revived by submitting the texts to certain "Going to the Water" purification rites, the nature of which I am sworn not to disclose.

The Night Has a Naked Soul

Cherokee magical spell written in the
Sequoyah Syllabary circa 1880

The Cherokee
Witchcraft-Sorcery Complex

Before describing the most conspicuous attributes of Cherokee witches and sorcerers (whose traits appear, at times, to be interchangeable and amorphous), I wish to dispell some popular misconceptions about the nature of these supernatural beings who have for centuries inhabited the Cherokee psyche. It should be strongly emphasized at the onset that the traditional Cherokee witch deviates from the standard fantasy of the "jealous hag flying on a broomstick," a model celebrated most commonly in European folklore.

In a Cherokee community, although it is generally agreed that knowledge about occult matters resides with elders, accusations of witchcraft may be directed at any individual who exhibits suspicious behavior. Because it is widely known that Cherokee witches, like those of the Seneca (Morgan [1851] 1972, 164–65), can assume many guises, it follows that no person (young, old, male, or female) can be totally exempt from this category.

The traditional Cherokee witch diverges incontrovertibly from its European counterpart in another respect. The Christianized view of the witch as a woeful creature who sells his or her soul to do Satan's bidding is a concept wholly alien to the Cherokee. Satanic covens of witches bound by the intractable "pactado con el Diablo" and trained in the black arts at *arbularias* (schools held by accomplished sorcerers) is largely a fabrication of southwestern and Mesoamerican folklore (cf. Simmons 1980, 40–44; Saler [1964] 1967, 30).

Although the aboriginal Cherokee may have subscribed to a hereditary priesthood caste, there is no ethnohistorical or folkloric evidence to suggest that Cherokee witches ever banded together in a "secret and

3

systematic organization with a novitiate fee and an initiation ceremony" as the Iroquois evidently did (Morgan [1851] 1972, 165). In contrast, the traditional Cherokee witch is undisputedly a solitary creature. The Cherokee witch lives alone, eats alone (fearful of being poisoned), and commits heinous acts alone, surreptitiously under the cover of darkness. Jealous and hypersensitive by nature, the Cherokee witch lives in the ever-fearful grip of being publicly exposed.

Cherokee folklore holds that a witch can be detected (and, therefore, controlled) by various methods. According to one Choctaw-Cherokee informant, the "bluish appearance of the face of a corpse in a coffin" offers irrefutable evidence that the deceased was a victim of witchcraft or sorcery (Tse:gi Ganv:hnawó:i field notes n.d.).

Among the western Cherokee, medicine men have been known to "doctor" dogs so that they can recognize witches who are approaching the house. During the eighteenth century the standard method employed by eastern Cherokee folk healers to "see" witches was to burn the dried bodies of field mice or shrews and rub the ashes in their eyes (Buttrick n.d., 2:56, cited in Fradkin 1990, 385).

Cherokee witches are known to keep a menagerie of "pets." According to another informant, any congregation of owls, dogs (type not specified), wolves, or lizards hovering around a particular residence of a dying person serves as prime facie evidence that the occupant within is a malevolent being (Tse:gi Ganv:hnawó:i field notes n.d.).

The association of lizards with witches here is curious because these reptiles most often form an intregal part of rain-making ceremonies, particularly the "spring lizard" (*Gyrinophilus porphyriticus* G.) (Mooney 1900, 307; Fradkin 1990, 139). It may be a borrowing from Muskogean folk beliefs. Among the Alabama and Koasati groups Swanton observes: "When a man became a witch these Indians believed he was full of lizards, which compelled the person of whom they had possession to kill someone every little while. If he did not they would begin to bite him and would finally devour him. Such a person could be cured, however, by undergoing a treatment to expel the lizards" (Swanton 1928, 635).

The punishment for practicing witchcraft has changed little over the centuries. The admonishment of Exod. 22:18, "Thou shall not suffer a witch to live," seems to have been embraced with singular fervor by most Native American societies. A telling example of this ageless prohibition can be seen at El Vallecito, a prehistoric Kumeyaay Indian rock art site located near Tecate, Mexico. Here, the eyes of the interested tourist can be directed toward a ghostly figure etched in granite with a spike drawn through its heart. Local legends assert that this spot is the resting place of a witch who was killed here and nailed down to his or her tomb for all eternity.

In keeping with such standards Cherokee witches could also expect to be executed summarily once their criminal natures were exposed. Witches, who are vulnerable to bullets, could be put to death either through natural means or by "lowering" their souls by magical rites (see texts 27–30).

The Seneca, according to Wallace, appear to have been more lenient than the Cherokee in this regard: "If a witch could be brought to confess and repent, by threats or physical torture or by such magical devices as burning the living heart of a blackbird, the witch's power would be broken. And, as a last resort, the witch could be killed" (Wallace 1972, 254–55).

A cursory survey of the ethnohistorical literature indicates that death was the standard punishment among Native American societies. Numerous eighteenth- and nineteenth-century accounts of random witch killings are recorded among the Chickasaw (Adair [1775] 1930), Natchez (Thwaites 1847, 425), the Miami (McCoy [1840], 1970, 97), and the Delaware (Miller 1994).

Swanton also records several incidences of witch killing among the Creek Indians. One account, in particular, captures the atmosphere of frenzied hatred that must have surrounded these public accusations: "As soon as it [was] announced that a man [was] acquainted with the work and dismal effects of the diabolical art . . . he was seized by a mob, tied to a tree with ropes, and lightwood piled around him and set on fire and he [was] burned to death with as little compunction or remorse of conscience as in the Roman inquisition" (Stiggins, cited in Swanton 1928, 632).

Even though laws were passed among the western Cherokee in 1824 forbidding the wanton killing of suspected witches, the activity appears to have continued unabated throughout the nineteenth century. Swanton, citing Hitchcock as his source, reports a similar situation that occurred among the Creek: "Formerly . . . the Indians have been known to knock old women regarded as witches on the head and throw them into the water. Now there is a law against it, but even last year an old woman was killed as a witch" (Swanton 1928, 632).

One might assume that witch hunts would abate in the twentieth century, particularly as those on Indian reservations became more attuned to the effects of psychological counseling, treatment in mental

institutions, and the use of therapeutic drugs. Despite the legal sanctions and the modern medical alternatives one occasionally reads in
ethnographic reports about the demise of a suspected witch in Native
American communities. As Shimony observes, most of these executions
take place "only while the witch is in animal guise (by shooting) or by
means of counter-witchcraft" (Shimony 1989, 160).

The Witch-Sorcerer Distinction

Much of our modern anthropological understanding of the complex psychosocial aspects of witchcraft-sorcery traditions in non-western tribal
societies can be traced to the pioneering studies of Evans-Pritchard
([1937] 1976) and Clyde Kluckhohn (1944). As valuable as these
monographs are in offering fundamental insights into the belief systems
of the Zande of Bahr-el-Ghazel and the Navajo Indians of the American Southwest, one cannot, without serious qualification, extend the
conclusions of these early ethnographers beyond these regions of study.
Thus, one of the critical problems facing researchers of supernatural
beliefs among Native American populations is the absence of all embracing categorical definitions that can be universally applied to all
practitioners of black magic (cf. Walker 1989, 13).

Illustrative of this point is Evans-Pritchard's highly influential and
often quoted theoretical argument that witches emanate evil essentially
through their "psychic" abilities: "A witch performs no rituals, utters no
spells, and possesses no medicines" (Evans-Pritchard [1937] 1976, 1). In
contrast, sorcerers were thought to rely solely upon "performed action"
(e.g., observable rituals, spoken incantations, and interventions from
spiritual sources) or what has been termed "magic rites with bad medicines" (1).

Although the analytical limitations of this generalization have been
widely discussed (Walker 1989, 1, 3), nevertheless, a number of more
recent studies of supernaturalism have continued to adopt his basic theoretical distinction. One notable example can be drawn from Mair's
survey: "The sorcerer uses material objects and the witch does not"
(Mair 1969, 23).

Although Evans-Pritchard's classic dichotomy appears useful in the
abstract, a careful analysis of the Cherokee folk beliefs about witchraft
and sorcery reveals that certain aspects of this categorial system are
untenable. Fogelson first observed these problems twenty years ago in
his admirable anthropological study of Cherokee magical practices:

"The sorcerer-witch distinction has only partial applicability in interpreting the Cherokee data" because "many of the Native terms today defy precise definitions" (Fogelson 1975, 119).

For instance, among the western Cherokee the ability to harm others by using one's "psychic" energy or focused thought is not confined exclusively to the realm of the witch. It is believed that a specialized class of conjurors exist who can sharpen their mental faculties to such a degree that they can inflict psychological or pathological harm upon an unsuspecting victim (Kilpatrick and Kilpatrick 1967b, 170). To prevent attacks from these *ane:li:sgi* ('those who think') a rather large corpus exists of protective charms usually designed under the rubric "to turn one aside" (see text 16).

Among the Cherokee, there is another area where the demarcation lines separating these two supernatural entities appears to blur. Closely related to the previous contention that only witches evince malevolent psychic abilties is the canonical tenet that witches are "born," whereas sorcerers are "made." It is true that many non-western tribal societies appear to view witches in this light and exhibit, as a result, a high degree of fatalism about the social redeemability of these nocturnal creatures. In ancient Mexico individuals born under a certain calendrical day-sign were thought by the Nahua-speaking Aztec to be irrevocably doomed to be a *nagual* (cf. Sahagun [1577] 1950–69). This same attitude, prevalent among contemporary Mestizo populations of Mesoamerica (Madsen 1989, 227) and among tribes in Central Africa (Mair 1969, 18–19) has been aptly summarized as "witches are made by God and it is He who gives them their fate at birth" (Aguirre Beltran 1963, 290).

Although most traditional Cherokees would agree that witches are, by and large, a product of nature, their folklore does allow that under certain circumstances an infant or even an adult may be transformed into a witch by following a strict, highly secretive regime. Historically, in northeastern Oklahoma and in the mountains of North Carolina, some newly born infants (particularly twins) were considered to be prime candidates for "witchhood." Prospective witches were immediately taken away from their mothers' breasts, kept in isolation for a set period of from seven to twenty-four days, and then nourished only on a "liquid of fermented hominy" or a "specially decocted herbal tea" (Mooney and Olbrechts 1932, 129–31; Fogelson 1975, 121–23).

The wife of a well-known Cherokee medicine man once commented upon this nefarious practice of "making" witches and offered a rationale for its decline: "Long ago the old people 'fixed' babies before they had nursed. Nowadays, there's a lack of witches because babies are inaccessible. They are so often born in hospitals" (Tse:gi Ganv:hnawó:i field notes n.d.).

According to Mooney and Olbrechts, a similar procedure could be conducted on an adult, male or female, who wished to acquire the supernatural powers of a witch, particularly the extraordinary ability to metamorphosize oneself into either animal or human form. The methodology here involved undergoing a strenuous fast for a period of four or seven days, then ingesting a specially prepared tea (Mooney and Olbrechts 1932, 30; Fogelson 1975, 122).

Frans Olbrechts provisionally identified the main ingredient of this "witch medicine" as *Sagittaria latifolia* W. Recent scholarship, however, has disproved Olbrechts's original finding. According to Witthoft, the four ingredients of this exotic brew (which were crushed and steeped in water) were algae collected from rocks in a mountain stream, phosphorescent wood extracted from a putrified stump, and two species of insect plants (*Cordyceps*) that contain the hallucinatory properties of ergot and lysergic acid diethylamide (1983, 71).

To the Cherokee mind this capacity for the magical transformation of physical form (whether human or animal) appears to be one of the most telling characteristics of the witch. The woods of northeastern Oklahoma are alive with stories of witches soaring through the sky as illuminating balls of fire, a trait thought by some ethnographers to have been introduced from European folklore (Parsons 1939, 1065–68) but which is found among widely dispersed Native American groups living in the southwest (Simmons 1980, 57–58) and in the northeast (Shimony 1989, 150).

It is believed by conservative Cherokees that witches can assume the form of lycanthropes (a practice somewhat akin to the Navajo *yenathósi* or 'shape shifter'). According to one Cherokee-Choctaw source, witches may even manifest as large flies that hover around a household, entering through the keyholes (Tse:gi Ganv:hnawó:i field notes n.d.).

No doubt, the perceived similarity between the nocturnal activities of malevolent beings and necrotic birds of prey led to the creation of the word, *tsi:sgili*, a generic Cherokee term that is used to designate both a witch and an owl (see text 25). Although there is general agreement among Cherokee scholars that both meanings are interchangeable, there seems to be some confusion in the literature about exactly which type of owl is being described here.

In their early ethnographic work Mooney and Olbrechts translate *tsi:sgili* as 'hoot owl' (1932, 29), a rendering that has been adopted by later researchers (Fogelson 1975, 120). This may be a linguistic oversight because the hoot owl and its confederate, the barred owl (*Strix varia* B.), are known among eastern and western Cherokee speakers as *u:gu:ghu* or a close variant (Kilpatrick and Kilpatrick, *English-Cherokee Dictionary* n.d.; cf. Alexander 1971, 77; Feeling and Pulte 1975, 205).

Fradkin, however, in a recent study of eastern Cherokee folk classificatory systems asserts that *tsi:sgili* means 'great horned owl' (*Bubu virginianus* Gmelin) (Fradkin 1990, 168–69). My own parents translated *tsi:sgili* as the 'long-eared owl' (*Asio wilsonianus*), a bird that, according to them, was both "hated and feared" because it was "held to be the commonest form into which witches and sorcerers transform themselves" (Kilpatrick and Kilpatrick 1970, 95 n. 54). This view finds further support from the ethnographic fieldwork conducted by John Witthoft (1946, 379).

To compound matters further, occasionally Cherokee witches have been known to carry out their malignant activities in the guise of the *wahuhi,* 'the screech owl' (*Otus asio* L.) (Kilpatrick and Kilpatrick 1967b, 159). Thus, it appears that the word *tsi:sgili* has metamorphized itself into an all-encompassing concept that is emblematic of all classes of owls.

Without question, the most feared and depraved forms of maleficence among the Cherokee are the vampiric creatures of the night who are variously known as *sv:no:yi ane:dó:hi* ('night walkers') and *kalona a:yéli:sgi* ('raven mockers') (see text 22). Like the Romanian *nosferatu,* it is believed that these specters of the "undead" renew their life force by devouring the blood, heart, or entrails of the living.

The only viable description of the Cherokee Raven Mocker comes from Mooney's 1900 account. Adjudged to be "of either sex" and "withered and old" as a consequence of adding "so many lives to their own," this fearsome birdlike creature "flies though the air in fiery shape, with arms outstretched like wings, and sparks trailing behind. . . . Every little while as he flies he makes a cry like the cry of a raven" (Mooney 1900, 401).

Raven Mockers are known to be particularly tormentful to their human prey. Like invisible beings they stealthfully enter a house of an ill person; then they "frighten and torment the sick man until they kill him. Sometimes to do this they even lift him from the bed and throw him on the floor" (Mooney 1900, 402).

According to Mooney, witches and Raven Mockers have an uneasy and adversarial relationship. Witches are known to be "jealous of the Raven Mockers and afraid to come into the same house with one. When at last a Raven Mocker dies, these other witches sometimes take revenge by digging up the body and abusing it" (1900, 402).

Although the belief in "Night Walkers" and "Raven Mockers" has been somewhat curtailed by the electronic monsters seen on today's television screens, some apprehension still persists among the Cherokee communities in northeastern Oklahoma about the plausible existence of these folkloric predators. One of this author's earliest childhood memories illustrates this fact.

In the late 1950s my father and I, on our way to Stilwell, Oklahoma, took a side excursion off Highway 100. The purpose of our trip into these remote woods was to see the grave of an aunt generations removed from my mother. "Nannie," as this distant relative was called, died sometime in the 1850s, and her mortal remains were interred in a curious wooden miniature of an Iroquoian longhouse, now ramshackle and decayed. Even more remarkable than the shape of her grave was the extreme isolation of the site located many miles from any human habitation. When I asked my father why Nannie "was buried all by herself" and "so far from everything," I was told the terrible truth—that she was rumored to have been a *kolana a:yélis:sgi* and "very evil." Thus, feared in death as much as in life, "Nannie" was forever banished from all human contact in observance of ancient Cherokee tradition.

Whereas the case of Nannie may illustrate the viability of local superstitions, it also demonstrates a more profound truth: to the Cherokee sensibility witches (whether male or female) represent the ultimate expression of human depravity and antisocial deviance. This is their cardinal trait.

A number of Native American groups seem to share this sentiment regarding the dangerous and destructive nature of witches. One of the more obvious examples comes from the Seneca language in which the word for witch, *'otha'*, literally means 'evil power' (Chafe 1963, 59). In the same vein the Chickasaw appellation for witch, *istabe*, can be translated as 'man-killer' (lit. *ishto* ['big'] *abi* ['to kill']) or even more telling as *hoollabe* ('spoilers of things sacred') (Swanton 1928, 634 n. 17).

According to Fogelson, the traditional Cherokee would normally regard a witch as a "counterfeit or pseudohuman being since humanity is but one among many guises that they assume in their incessant metamorphosis and in their parasitic relationship to the Cherokee community" (Fogelson 1975, 128). Because witches violate the sanctions of Cherokee morality, Fogelson suggests that witches are considered by many Cherokees as "dead" or "nonpersons" (Fogelson 1979, 87).

This Cherokee attitude of extreme abhorrence, however, is not universally shared. According to Mair, the Zande of the Sudan "are exceptional because they think of witches as ordinary persons and have not elaborated an image of the witch as the enemy of all good men and the epitome of evil" (Mair 1969, 18). Spindler observed an even more curious situation among the Menominee of the Great Lakes where "the witch (or the person who performs acts of witchcraft at times) can be a respected elder" (Spindler 1989, 40).

Another defining characteristic of the Cherokee witch mentioned in Fogelson's article but not fully elaborated upon is the idea that these malevolent creatures are generally regarded as "violators of social space." Throughout my childhood in Oklahoma I heard numerous eyewitness accounts of witch sightings. Preserved either through the exchange of idle gossip or through the medium of the well-crafted *u:sghwanighdi* ('amazing') story, I was told how witches appeared as glowing balls of fire and perched themselves atop the church steeple or how, in human form, they entered a patient's hospital room. One informant described how his father "used to chase off a Mockingbird which came at night and sang in a Chinaberry tree near the house where the informant, as a child, lay ill with diabetes" (Tse:gi Ganv:hnawó:i field notes n.d.)

What binds these incredible narratives together is the belief that the parasitic nature of witches drives them to invade and despoil socially sanctioned areas (churches, hospitals, cemetaries, private homes, etc.). Thus, the Cherokee witch represents a supernatural force beyond social control. This perceived threat to the social order is why Cherokee communities regard their witches with such an abiding sense of fear and disdain.

Sorcerers

Like the Seneca (Shimony 1989, 144), the Cherokee do not recognize the English term *sorcerer*. Instead, they prefer to employ several interrelated terms that mean 'conjuror.' One of the terms, which might have been confected during the nineteenth century because it is used often in translations of the Old and New Testaments, is *ado:ni:sgi* (pl. *dina:*

donisgi). Corrupted by my own infelicitous translation, the concept of 'sorcery' might be approximated by the phrase *ado:naltdóho:i* ('he [habitually] goes about conjuring') (see Reyburn 1953, 178).

Another term used more often to denote someone who uses magical abilities for ill purpose is *dida:hnese:sgi* (lit. 'putter-in and drawer-out of them'). This term is particularly descriptive of the dynamics of this practitioner's technique. In Cherokee metaphysics supernatural illness usually operates through some magical exchange of vital forces (e.g., "shooting" a magical object into the victim's physical body [texts 13–14] or extracting the life energies ('soul loss') directly from the victim (text 25).

Besides these generic terms, there are a number of cognate designations for sorcererlike entities. One of these terms is *imprecator*, which Mooney first glossed as 'evil, speaker of it, he' (Mooney 1891, 384). Fogelson, in his otherwise perceptive article, mistakenly asserts that this term is restricted only to the eastern Cherokee (1975, 124).

Recently, I encountered several western Cherokee texts of nineteenth-century vintage at the Beinecke Rare Book Library that are devoted to nullifying the effects of an "imprecator." To ward off *unayehi:sdi* ('frightful') *iyanadawedehi* ('sayers') as they are called in these texts, it is recommended that a rarified species of ancient tobacco be rolled in the hand while one recites the appropriate lines. The ritual is to be enacted early in the morning on the bank of a flowing stream.

While perusing the same collection, I encountered another possible colloquialism for conjuror. In a text captioned "To Learn Medicine" the reciter is advised that by employing this particular spell, he or she may become a *ditsiqwaniyo:hihi* ('one who gambles'). It is only conjecture, of course, but this rarely employed word may be an archaism. "A gambler" may somehow be related to the seventeenth-century term, *juggler* (Fr. *jongleur*), first popularized by the French Jesuits to denote a conjuror. This synonymous term enjoyed rather wide coinage among the Illinois (Callender 1978, 677), the Menominee (Spindler 1989, 44, 47) and the Natchez (Charlevoix 1851, cited in Swanton 1911).

In the present collection one encounters the euphemism, *gegó:nelvhi* ('to have been put in this condition'), which equates with the verb, *conjured* (see text 13). Undoubtedly, other such circumlocutions were employed to describe the state of bewitchment.

The final term dealt with here, *ada:wé:hi* ('wizards'), which appears in text 1 and appears frequently throughout the collection, refers to long-dead, highly revered virtuosi of magic. Fogelson (1975) is quite correct in his assessment that no Cherokee magician living in the modern age would dare boast of having comparable supernatural powers.

Although one might inherit or acquire the status of a witch, it is generally held by Cherokee traditionalists that the esoteric secrets of the sorcerer can only be learned through a lengthy apprenticeship with a master practitioner. Esoteric knowledge about how to attract women, how to make it rain, or how to take a human life had for centuries been orally transmitted from master to student and then committed to memory. The invention of the Sequoyan script, no doubt, greatly facilitated this learning process by creating a writing system that could effectively preserve this sacred information.

In addition to this specialized training aspiring Cherokee conjurors needed spiritual guidance to fulfill their destinies. Unique in this regard is the following Cherokee *i:gawé:sdi*, or magical text. Its primary purpose appears to be to assist apprentice conjurors in learning their craft. This formula was found in the personal effects of Uwe:da:sad(h)i Sa:wali, the great-uncle of my late mother, who was not only a medicine man of some renown in northeastern Oklahoma but was also an active member of the Keetoowah, or Black Hawk, Society, a traditionalist organization peopled by full-blood Cherokees. Judging from the style of the caligraphy as well as the condition of the paper, this formula was recorded during the late nineteenth century:

Text 1 "To Learn Conjuroring"

Instructions

ani:da:wé:hi	*gohú:sdi*	*unada:nohi:sedi:i*
wizards	something	to tell you, then

yodu:lihá	*adela:qwasdiyi*	*sv:no:yi*
if you want	to learn	night

galo:hisdi i:gi		*gohú:sdi*	*ase:qwo*
you have to go through it		something	in vain

galo:hisdi i:gi	*gohú:sdi*	*naddé:losvna*
you have to go through it	something	without one knowing, it

yegi   *sv:no:yi*   *galo:hisdi i:gi*
[emphasis]   night   you have to go through it

hiʔaʔ   *tsigo:hwé:la*
this   it is written

Free Translation

If you want to learn, if you want the wizards to tell you something, you have to go through it at night. If something is in vain [your magic is turned back], you have to go through it. You have to do it at night. It is written this way.

Spell

nv:no:hi   *uné:gv*   *aquadé:dowadi*
path   white   I am heading down

o:dali   *uné:gv*   *sdo:yi*   *hwi:tsigadi*
mountain   white   hard as I can   I am going

hiʔaʔ *iyú:sdi* *diquadóidú*   ✕
this   kind   I am named   [reciter says name]

nv:no:hi   *gigagé:*   *aquadé:dowadi*
path   red, it   I am heading down

o:dali   *gv:hnáge* *sdo:yi*   *hwi:tsigadi*
mountain   black, it as hard as I can   I am going

gahligwo:gine   *galúlohi*   *ane:hi*
seventh   heaven   where they live

ani:sgaya   *tsunasdí:i*   *ani:da:wé:hi*
men   small ones   wizards

dogatsi:sgalawi:sdihidi
side by side

nigvne:hi   *ha!*   *ditsa:yvwi*
where they live ha!   clan, your

usdá:gali   *sv:dó:hi*
climber   walker

wo:tsidadi   *nv:no:hi*   *gigagé:*
we are going path   red, it

aline:tluni:ga
they have come to rejoice [to make sounds with their mouths]

gawo:hilosi:ga
they have come to answer

nv:no:hi   *gv:hnáge:*   *aline:tluni:ga*
path   black   they have just come to rejoice [to make
                                  sounds with their mouths]

gawo:hilosi:ga
they have come to answer.

Free Translation

I am heading down the white path.
I'm going as hard as I can to the white mountain.
[This kind I am named]
I am heading down the red path.
I'm going as hard as I can to the black mountain.
[I'm going to] the seventh heaven where they're from.
The Little Men, wizards, side by side, where they live.
Ha! Clan climber-walker!
We're going down the red path.
They've just come to rejoice!
They've just come to answer!
[We're going down to] the black path.
They've just come to rejoice!
They've just come to answer

Although most Cherokee practitioners of magic are male, the profession does have its female counterparts (see texts 6 and 10). Even though they may undergo metamorphosis through the enactment of specialized rituals, Cherokee conjurors, unlike witches, are basically thought to be *yv:wi*, or 'human.'

As such, they are generally circumspect about using their magical abilities, and they normally exhibit great care in exercising their esoteric powers. This judicious degree of restraint contrasts sharply with the "avowedly contracultural and antisocial activity" of the witch, who "lacks most of these control features" (Fogelson 1975, 117) and as such creates one of the more reliable theoretical distinctions that one can make between Cherokee witches and sorcerers.

The Transmission of Magic

To grasp fully the dynamics of witchcraft and sorcery as Cherokee traditionalists practice it one must recognize that its dynamics are intimately tied to certain powerful metaphysical concepts. As cited earlier, a key principle of these occult activities involves the magical exchange of vital energies.

Most of these mystical transactions are targeted to affect the proper functioning of what might be termed the human soul. The Cherokee notion of this immaterial essence differs considerably from the Christianized view.

The Cherokee word for soul is *ada:n(v)do*ʔ. Its semantic meaning, deconstructed from its root, *adaʔnv́ a*, indicates that someone or something is in transit, moving from place to place (cf. Feeling and Pulte 1975, 6). This transitory vision of this mutable and mobile essence has its origins, according to Fogelson, in the aboriginal Cherokee belief that four primal animate life forces emanate from the human body.

The first of these quadripartite souls, which Fogelson terms *the soul of consciousness*, is centered "in the head or throat and is associated with saliva" (Fogelson 1979, 90). He then identifies the remaining three 'vital essences' as the "hepatic soul" located "in the liver"; the "visceral soul" "located in the flesh" and "associated with blood"; and, finally, the "osseous soul," which "resides in the bones and is associated with sperm"(90). This indigenous metaphysical understanding of multiple life forces obviously wars against the Augustian vision of the soul as *unus ego animus*, the transcendent logocentric object of inner experience, the self-conscious spiritual mass.

This belief in the multiplicity of souls was, of course, not confined to the Cherokee but was a widespread phenomenon among the indigenous peoples of the Americas. According to Le Jeune's relation of 1639, the Huron of the St. Lawrence believed in the existence of "several souls" (Thwaites 1847, 376). Furthermore, the Narragansett Indians of the northeastern United States apparently believed in two distinct spiritual components (Simmons 1978, 192, citing Williams 1936, 130, 137).

In the plains region the Lakota Sioux have long maintained a traditional belief that the human spirit is composed of certain vital integral elements: the *nagi, niya, sicun,* and, perhaps, the *taku skan skan,* as well (DeMallie, Jahner, and Walker 1980, 72, citing James Walker). More recent ethnographic research conducted among the Alaskan Tlingit also reveals a long-standing metaphysical belief in two or more spiritual essences (Kan 1989, 52–53).

One can trace the same belief system to ancient Mexico as well. There is considerable ethnohistorical evidence that the Nahua-speaking Aztecs of Tenochtitlán believed in a triad of vital forces, the *tonalli, teyolia,* and *ihiyotl,* which kept the human body in balance (Lopez Austin 1988, 1:313–16; Ortiz de Montellano 1990, 55–67).

Among the western Cherokee modern folk healers seem to have moderated not only their metaphysical but also their anatomical views of the soul to coincide more closely with their reading of the scripture. One elderly Cherokee medicine man interviewed by my late father during the early 1960s expressed the conviction that the human soul was "half as large as a thumb" and was situated "inside the heart" (Tse:gi Ganv:hnawó:i field notes n.d.).

Soul Loss

Coupled to this concept of the soul as a multivariate and free-ranging essence is the idea that this life-nurturing force can be snatched from the body by some menacing outside agent, particularly during periods of unconsciousness, resulting in illness or death. The phenomenon of *soul loss* has been widely documented cross-culturally (see Clements 1932; Sigerist 1951; and Lewis 1971). Judging from the large number of ethnographic descriptions, this ancient belief was extremely prevalent among Native American societies (see Le Jeune's 1636 account of the Huron cited in Thwaites 1847, 376, 378, and the more recent anthropologically oriented discussions about the Menominee [Spindler 1989, 44], Maliseat-Passaquoddy [Erickson 1978, 133], Creek [Swanton 1928, 654–55], Cheyenne [Hoebel 1960, 86], Seminole [Hudson 1976, 344], and the Paviotso [Parker 1938, 37, 41]).

Soul loss seems to be related to the malady known as *susto*, a psychological disorder that has been widely documented in Mexico and in Latin America as well (Kiev 1968; Rubel, O'Nell, and Collado-Ardon, 1984). In this context, however, the affliction is thought to be caused by sudden fright or trauma, which may or may not have a supernatural origin.

The Cherokees, like many other Native American societies, were well attuned to the metaphysical affliction of soul loss although, apparently, they did not endorse the belief that the soul wanders from the body during sleep (Mooney and Olbrechts 1932, 141). To the Cherokee mind the involuntary loss of one's vital life force most often manifested as a psychopathological condition of abject melancholia known as *uhí:soʔdí* ('the blue'), which has been described as "a state of ecstatic yearning" somewhat akin to a depressive form of lovesickness (Kilpatrick and Kilpatrick 1964, 191) (see text 15). According to Siquinid, a Cherokee-Natchez Baptist minister and medicine man who lived in northeastern Oklahoma, "there is a big difference between mere loneliness and *uhí:soʔdí*. The difference is unmistakable" (Tse:gi Ganv:hnawó:i field notes n.d.).

According to Cherokee folk belief, human souls can, on occasion, be "ravaged" or taken hostage through the supernatural machinations of a *tsi:sgili* or a *dida:hnese:sgi* (Mooney and Olbrechts 1932, 16). One maniacal strategem employed by Cherokee conjurors to ensure the total extinction of an adversary involves burying the victim's captured soul either underground (see text 30a) or dispelling it "'out west' in the Nightland" (Mooney and Olbrechts 1932, 141). In such cases the daunting task of thwarting these evil designs and recapturing a displaced soul could only be accomplished by a highly experienced *dida:hnvwi:sgi* ('curer of them').

Object Intrusion

To the Cherokee traditionalist the phenomenon of *Hexenschuss*, or 'object intrusion,' represents another specific manifestation of magical intervention by a witch or a conjuror. This folk belief that psychological discomfort or pathological illness can be inflicted by magically introjecting objects or forces into a victim's body appears to be exceedingly widespread. According to Sigerist, "It is almost universal on the American continent, is found in northeastern Siberia, southeastern Asia, Australia and New Zealand, is encountered in Africa in spots and almost universally in European folklore" (Sigerist 1951, 128). The belief in object intrusion must be of considerable antiquity because the Papyrus Leiden records that the ancient Egyptians were bothered by demonic entities who attempted to take spiritual possession of infants by shooting invisible arrows into the child's body (Papyrus Leiden, 346, 1.5, cited in Sigerist 1951, 274).

The magical technique of inserting an injurious, foreign object into a victim appears to vary widely in the literature. In ancient Mexico the Nahua-speaking Aztec believed that their *Tlalatetecolo* ('owl men' [sorcerers]) enjoyed the power to cast spells mentally into the bodies of their victims, which would then materialize as sharp fragments of bone or obsidian (Ortiz de Montellano 1990, 141). During the seventeenth century the Huron Indians were evidently troubled by witches who could perform similar feats of magic (Shimony 1989, 145).

The residue of such beliefs can be found among the Muskogean-speaking tribes in the southeastern United States:

> From a Texas Alabama I learned that a witch operated by taking a small raveling of wool which he talked to and blew upon and then sent through the air to the person he wished to injure. It would go into this person and prevent him from breathing, or hurt him in some other way, so as to endanger his life unless the trouble was located. (Swanton 1928, 634)

Apparently, not all "object intrusion" was accomplished by mental projection. According to Sigerist, vengeful sorcerers in Melanesia were known to infect their victims by using a "ghost-shooter," a type of bamboo blowgun containing the ground bones of a corpse, leaves, and other unidentified by-products (Sigerist 1951, 129). Even more astounding is the Yagua conjurer of Peru who, according to the same source, carries within his body a host of lethal darts that he can extract from his skin by smoking his whole body and, if provocation warrants it, hurl into the body of his victim (Sigerist 1951, 129).

Evidently, it was commonly held that a sorcerer could harm a victim from a considerable distance. An extreme case of this belief appears to have existed among the Creek Indians during the nineteenth century: "They firmly believe that their Indian enemies have the power of shooting them as they lie asleep, at a distance of 500 miles. They often complain of having been shot by a Choctaw or Chickasaw from the midst of these nations" (Swanson 1928, 654).

Historically, one effective countermeasure to remove foreign, magically placed objects involved a folk healer who performed therapeutic surgery on the wound by using an array of hollowed-out tubes, bones, or animal horns as sucking devices. Cherokee curers living in the nineteenth century carved their surgical instruments out of buffalo or cow horns (Mooney and Olbrechts 1932, 73).

Other curing techniques thought to be effective against object intrusion involved spraying the patient's body with one's breath, employing emetics or physical massage, or driving out the offending substance through songs and incantations (cf. Parker's survey of shamanism among the Great Basin tribes [1938, 124]).

Occasionally, the veracity of these magical rites was called into question, particularly by early white observers. A notable critic, French missionary Father Le Petit, characterized the eighteenth-century Natchez folk healers as "charlatans." He reports on their acts of legerdemain:

> Sometimes they cut, with a flint, the part afflicted by the malady, and then suck out all the blood they can draw from it, and in returning it immediately into a dish, they at the same time spit out a little piece of wood, or straw, or feather, which they have concealed under the tongue. (Le Petit in Thwaites 1847, 436)

Mindful of Father Le Petit's charge, a review of the ethnographic literature on these curing rites reveals an astounding range of magical substances reportedly retrieved from a patient's body. From two accounts of the Cheyenne healing rituals Grinnell reports that folk healers recovered buffalo hair, stones, and lizards from their victims, whereas Hoebel, in a later study, lists hair balls, a small feather, a crystal fragment, and even a thorn! (Grinnell 1923, 2:130; Hoebel 1960, 88). Matilda Coxe Stevenson, in her monograph on the ethnobotany of the Zuni (1915, 40), lists a remarkable store of objects extracted from victims' bellies: pebbles, bits of blankets, and even yards of yarn!

Among the Cherokee a favorite missile of conjurors was the *ga:dhidv*, which could take a variety of material forms: splinters of wood, strings, and even the bodies of insects. Cherokee thaumaturgy distinguishes quite clearly between wounds inflicted by an actual gunshot and projectiles that have been sent by supernatural forces. Slippery elm bark is the standard remedy to treat bullet injuries, whereas certain medicinal remedies, notably concoctions of sassafras, polk root, and cornmeal, are used to treat *ga:dhidv* cases.

The sucking horn, the favorite surgical implement of the nineteenth-century Cherokee curer, has long become obsolete. As texts 13 and 14 attest, modern Cherokee folk healers now favor using poultices to absorb magical substances.

Imitative and Contagious Magic

Although the present set of texts contains little information on the matter, there is ample evidence to suggest that the aboriginal Cherokee engaged in acts of "imitative" as well as "contagious" magic. As outlined in Frazer's classic treatise, *The Golden Bough*, imitative magic might generally be defined as a set of mimetic actions designed to transfer the empowering supernatural properties of plants, animals, or inanimate entities to other human beings. Laboring under this "like produces like" principle, a man might carry a charm of snake fangs around his neck to protect him from actual snakebite.

One of the most well-known strategies of imitative magic, widely employed in the voodoo traditions of the Afro-Caribbean, was to make an effigy or doll, of the intended victim. Believers thought that torturing this smaller image would transfer the actual pain to its living counterpart. Although the making of human effigies or "witch" dolls is a well-documented feature among the Menominee (Spindler 1989, 49–50), Iroquois (Shimony 1989, 148), Seminole (Howard and Lena 1984, 94–95), and the Pueblo cultures (Ellis 1989, 209), little evidence exists that the Cherokee historically engaged in such activity.

Certainly, there is very little mention of this practice in the shamanistic texts of the western Cherokee. When surveying the published literature, I discovered only two statements that might possibly be construed as evidence for effigy making. Both examples were extracted from love-attracting formulae: "Already You and I have just come to keep her image!" (Kilpatrick and Kilpatrick 1965, 60), and "I have just come to make an image of You!" (Kilpatrick and Kilpatrick 1970, 97). As such, these proclamations might more easily be regarded as expressions of ardent desire on the part of the reciter than actual incidents during which imitative magic was employed.

A more conspicuous feature, however, can be noted in magical texts of both the eastern and western Cherokee. Often an introductory section appears, that is kept separate from the body of the incantation in which the reciter is obligated to proclaim aloud the name of the targeted victim/patient and his or her appropriate clan. In my estimation the primary function of this "naming" procedure is to operate as a "focusing" device, allowing reciters to direct their psychic energies toward the beneficary of the magic.

I acknowledge here (following Mooney's lead), however, that it may, in effect, have a secondary function as a form of imitative magic. Mooney (1891) was the first ethnographer to observe the critical importance that the Cherokees of the historic past placed on their personal names: "The Indian regards his name, not as a mere label, but as a distinct part of his personality, just as much as are his eyes, or his teeth, and believes that injury will result as surely from the malicious handling of his name or from a wound inflicted on any part of his physical organism" (Mooney 1891, 343). If one is to believe Mooney's account, the aboriginal Cherokee believed that through the power of imitative magic one could "capture" or "hold onto" an individual's personality by reciting a particular name aloud and then by cursing it actually harm that individual.

In contrast to the paucity of evidence surrounding the use of homoepathic modes of vitalizing magic considerable proof exists that Cherokee witches and sorcerers traditionally employed "contagious" magic defined by Frazer as "the magical sympathy which is supposed to exist between a man and any severed portion of his person, such as his hair or nails; so that whoever gets possession . . . may work his will, at any distance, upon the person from whom they were cut" (Frazer [1890] 1959, 62).

In ancient Mexico Aztec sorcerers highly prized the severed left forearms of women who had died in childbirth as potent weapons to cripple, paralyze, or otherwise anesthetize their victims (Sahagun [1577] 1950–69, 4:101–6), In a similar vein Cherokee conjurors favored collecting the moist saliva of their victims. To gain possession of a person's spittle bestowed upon the conjuror "power over the life of the man himself" (Mooney 1891, 392).

In northeastern Oklahoma *tsi:sgilis* were rumored to keep an assemblage of strands of hair taken from various animals and from humans. Using these extracted follicles, these witches could then transform themselves into the exact shape of the hair's owner (Tse:gi Ganv: hnawó:i field notes n.d.).

It should be noted that although the majority of the texts collected in this book are corrective measures against witches, the transmission of harmful forms of magic is not confined to one class of evildoers. Just as witches can be motivated to inflict harm so, too, can sorcerers.

In one vital sense a number of these "exchange" dynamics (particularly soul loss/gain and object intrusion/extraction) intimately link the witch and the sorcerer in a codependent role. Usually, the dynamic is simple: the witch manifests a spell on a victim, and the sorcerer, for a fee, heals the patient. Sometimes, however, the situation warrants more drastic measures. As texts 29 and 30 suggest, the conjuror, feeling threatened by the source of the trouble, may resolve not only to "turn back" the magic but also to destroy the witch.

Given the fact that some Cherokee conjurors ('thinkers') are known to possess the same witchlike powers mentally to cripple or to kill, one can easily observe how these traditional roles become blurred during bouts of "psychic warfare" involving the conveyance and counterconveyance of lethal magic. Viewed in this light, these polarized categories of *witch* as 'bringer of chaos' and *sorcerer* as 'restorer of order' begin to evaporate, theoretical distinctions begin to break down, and the two entities of witch and sorcerer become almost indistinguishable.

2

Transformational Language

Of the more than 150,000 people who claim membership in the Cherokee Nation of Oklahoma it has been estimated that only about 15,000 can speak their native language, and of that group, perhaps no more than one-half can actually read or write in the Sequoyah syllabary. Today, among the Oklahoma Cherokee the use of the Sequoyah syllabary is restricted, by and large, to ceremonial purposes such as the recitation of the *idi:gawé:sdi*. Occasionally, passages from the Cherokee New Testament are read aloud from the syllabary during community church services.

Despite this erosion of native literacy a substantial number of Cherokee *idi:gawé:sdi* have been preserved in dime store blue-lined ledger notebooks. These manuscripts are referred to by the Cherokees themselves as *nv:wo:dhi digo:hwé:li*, or medicine books. Besides these bound volumes of *idi:gawé:sdi,* one also finds occasional arcane scribblings on the backs of Civil War enlistment papers, children's writing tablets, and odd bits of cardboard.

Fragments of these esoteric texts have also come to light in the most unlikely places: squirreled away in the trunks of dead trees, buried in jars beneath surreptitiously marked stones, or kept as family heirlooms by the descendants of these medicine men, who become terribly evasive when asked by strangers about the existence of such manuscripts. One suspects that a considerable number of these medicine books may yet be hidden away in rural northeastern Oklahoma or in the Smokey Mountain region of Tennessee and North Carolina.

Although most Cherokee folk healers retain an arsenal of these magicomedical formulas with which to service their clientele, not all Cherokee magic is up-to-date. For example, the need to empower hunting and fishing skills has been vitiated by twentieth-century technology. Although examples of these hunting songs still exist, few conjurors bother to retain them in their modern repertoires.

Despite the Herculean efforts of my predecessors a large number of Cherokee *idi:gawé:sdi* remain at this date untranslated in the archives of the Smithsonian and the American Philosophical Society and in the Western Americana collection of the Bienecke Rare Book library at Yale University. The main difficulty in translating the idi:gawé:sdi results from the fact that Cherokee traditionalists invariably employ a highly specialized vocabulary to codify their spells, one that is replete with ritualisms, archaisms, loan words, and unusual verb forms. As a result, it has been observed that the *transformational language* employed by the *dida:hnese:sgi* ('putter-in and drawer-out of them') can bear as little resemblance to ordinary Cherokee discourse as Chaucer's Old English does to the writings of James Joyce (Kilpatrick and Kilpatrick 1965, 49).

The purpose of 'transformational language' in the Cherokee context appears to be twofold. First, this specialized Cherokee vernacular is clearly designed to baffle the uninitiated reader and, thus, cloak the text in a protective layer of secrecy. Second, and perhaps most importantly, conjurors use this hyperbolic language to dramatize the extraordinary nature of their intent and to focus on their thoughts. For only when their magic has become potent, or "remade," can the text become "alive" with supernatural power. These two "strategies of empowerment" are employed in several ways.

Limits of Knowledge

The fact that Cherokee shamanistic texts are so notoriously difficult to translate qualifies them, in a sense, to be regarded as a form of cryptography, "a secret language whose meanings can only be deciphered by those who have the key and thus are initiated into the code" (Staller 1994, 335). Among the western Cherokee this conscious use of a specialized and circumspect language is highly indicative of the aura of secrecy that surrounds the dissemination of arcane knowledge.

Folk beliefs in magic, in effect, function on two sociological levels: first, as a closed informational system from which the uninitiated are barred; second, as a source of ethnic identity for its membership. Cherokee conjurors cloak much of their tribal magic in euphemisms and are disinclined to discuss the secrets of their profession with anyone except another initiated practitioner. Within their inner circle, however, they may exchange trade secrets among peers, discussing the best places "to work" ("to conjure") or they may speak about cases they "worked" on.

I experienced a measure of this exclusivity recently from one of my principal informants, a Cherokee male in his early sixties. One day while we were in his home, L. boasted that he "had never been sick or had a cold." When I asked him about the source of his vigorous health, he informed me that for a long time he had supplemented his diet with a special tonic that he had learned to concoct from his uncle, a medicine man in Oklahoma. With my scientific curiosity piqued I asked L. to share his secret recipe with me. He, of course, refused.

The Power of Thought

Human thought is considered to be the primary vehicle of transformation in the Cherokee shamanistic literature. In the western Cherokee traditions of witchcraft and sorcery it is those individuals who think evil thoughts, *ane:li:sgi,* who are considered to be the primary cause of illness.

Akin to other Native American belief systems, Cherokees share the conviction that human thought can become supremely powerful if it can be focused and directed at some target. Assuming that this idea is valid, the critical question remains: How do individuals actualize magic by using their mental agencies?

The charismatic process of influencing human behavior through magical means is complex, agonistic, and fraught with problems. At the very least, ordinary realities must be subsumed, reordered, or transcended by a heightened atmosphere of mystical theatricality.

Instigators of spells must first achieve an altered state of perception before they can effect their wills upon others, manipulate physical environments, or communicate with supernatural forces. To "make the magic come alive" in this ecstatic state demands that ritual specialists be skilled enough to integrate potentially disruptive, violent, and creative forces once they are granted to them.

The vehicle of language serves two vital functions: first, the written text constitutes a set of ordered meanings that allows the reciter access to a superb compendium of Cherokee metaphysical insights, a source of generational knowledge about esoteria. Thus, the words of the incantation serve as an organizing mechanism to help the practitioner of magic handle paranormal phenomena through all stages of the ritual performance.

Second, heightened by a hyperbolic turn of phrase, this specialized vernacular allows reciters to dramatize the effect of the spell, to enliven the presence of spirits, and to reimagine the world in exponentially more powerful terms. By intoning the words of the incantation reciters create a nascent spatial dimension, a psychic landscape where the targeted actors and objects can be identified and placed in a new relationship to them. This allows enchanters to sharpen their thought processes and to "pinpoint" their psychic energies toward patients/victims.

The Cherokee belief in the powerful, concretizing dimension of ritualistic language is equally shared by other Native American groups. Navajo phenomenology, in particular, celebrates the all-encompassing, generative nature of ritualistic words: "Ritual language does not describe how things are; it determines how they will be. Ritual language is not impotent; it is powerful. It commands, compels, organizes, transforms and restores. It disperses evil, reverses disorder, neutralizes pain, overcomes fear, eliminates illness, relieves anxiety, restores order, health, and well-being" (Witherspoon 1977, 34).

According to Swanton (1928), Creek practioners of magical songs and formulae, the *isti poskalgi* ('fasting men'), expressed a similar belief in the innate potency of their ritualistic invocations to evoke miraculous states: "'By a word' a man could stand aside in the warpath and render himself invisible to the enemies. 'By a word' a man could even condense the whole world in such a way that he could go around it in four steps" (Swanton 1928, 503).

The collection of *idi:gawé:sdi* presented here represent more than a blueprint of the most efficacious words, phrases, and physical procedures known to remedy a particular situation. They represent the prime mechanism for generating and unleashing concentrated mental energy. This is why *idi:gawé:sdi* assume such a primacy among Cherokee practitioners of magic.

In contrast to the spontaneous and infinitely creative manifestations of ordinary human conversation transformational language is by its nature conservative, socially restricted, grounded in tradition, hallowed, and word-specific. It has been noted that the Cherokee folk healer regards the *idi:gawé:sdi* with such an air of inviolability and awe that "a text that has descended to him through tradition he may not knowingly alter, though he may not fully understand what he is saying" (Kilpatrick and Kilpatrick 1967b, 7). In fact, one medicine man opined that some formulae are so inherently "strong" that the same text can be used to treat as many as seven different diseases (Tse:gi Ganv:hnawó:i field notes n.d.).

This situation stands in stark contrast to the physical actions that may accompany the recitation of the text. These activities, known as the *igv́:n(e)dhi* ('to do something, one'), often involve smoking a pipe, making stylized movements through space, imitating spirit calls, and so forth. Unlike the text, here the reciter is free to modify, curtail any portion of, or even completely dispense with these physical adjunctives.

Structure of the Texts

Thus far, the studies that have been conducted on the Cherokee *idi:gawé:sdi* demonstrate that the shamanistic texts authored by the eastern band living in North Carolina exhibit marked stylistic differences from the writings of their western counterparts who live in northeastern Oklahoma. The eastern Cherokee have a more rigid and formal quality to the recitations and praxis of their rituals, whereas the shamanistic texts of the western Cherokee "teem with cabalistic abbreviations, eccentric spellings, and dialectal variants" (Kilpatrick and Kilpatrick 1970, 85). One might suspect that the literary balkanization perceived in the western Cherokee texts is a result of the psychic trauma brought on by their historic removal from the steadfast traditions of their homeland.

Despite these regional stylistic and dialectical differences all *idi:gawé: sdi* seem to share a number of structural principles in common. Indeed, historically, it was the perceived similarities in theoretical design and traditional phraseology that allowed noviate medicine men to memorize these intricate and sometimes lengthy formulae from their mentors at one sitting. According to Mooney, "a candidate for the priesthood" would be sorely judged by his ability to absorb quickly the intricacies of the incantation, and "one who failed to remember after the first hearing was not worthy to be accounted a shaman" (Mooney 1891, 309).

The exegesis of the Cherokee *idi:gawé:sdi* reveals that these texts, distilled of their poetic complexities, ecstatic mysticism, and complicated staging, can be readily analyzed as a four-part methodology involving the following mechanisms:

1. An identity tag used to focus the magic by specifying the patient by name and clan affiliation

2. An invocation of supernatural forces or declaration of self-affirmed powers by the reciter

3. The actualization of magic through the use of time-conflating adverbial modifiers and the inducement of psychological states through the vehicle of color symbolism

4. The stabilization or homeostasis of the spell achieved through imperative commands or through statements involving negative reinforcement.

In addition, it is quite common to encounter additional "buttressing" devices used to strengthen the spell. The most common of these prescriptive measures involves vocalizing the formulae a specified number of times (usually four or seven repetitions) or timing the ritual performance to coincide with certain potent nocturnal or diurnal intervals.

Identity Tag

A large number of Cherokee *idi:gawé:sdi* contain a standardized mechanism to identify not only the patient but also his clan affiliation. Sometimes inserted at the beginning of a spell (cf. text 10), in its middle (cf. text 1), or occasionally at its conclusion (cf. texts 26 and 31), this identity tag usually takes the form of two simple declarative statements:

digwadó:idú   *ditlidóidú*
this is my name   these are my people

One can easily understand the utility of identifying the principle beneficiary of the metaphysical exercise. It has been observed, however, that this "precise identification" not only "pinpoints" the name and the clan of an individual but also "lays bare the essence of his personality upon which spiritual action may be taken" (Kilpatrick and Kilpatrick 1967b, 189 n. 5).

Thus, it should be stressed that specificity is the key element to the shamanistic healing dynamic. To the Cherokee mind the act of naming something, *-ado-*, allows a revitalized mental image to be created. As a result, this metaphysical process "involves an emotional intensification and condensation of datum of experience" (Gingerich 1987, 104).

Mooney (1891) offers the additional explanation that the Cherokees placed special importance upon their personal names. In cases of serious illness shamans might conclude that the failure of their magic could be traced to the contamination of their clients' names. To remedy this situation the shaman "accordingly goes to water, with appropriate ceremonies, and christens the patient with a new name, by which he is henceforth to be known" (Mooney 1891, 343).

A psychological strategy employed frequently in eastern Cherokee medicinal texts is for the reciter to visualize that some healing spirit has triumphantly taken away the illness from a patient's body and "put it somewhere" (Mooney 1891, 346). By assigning the illness to some remote, unspecified locale the threatening agent is displaced, stripped of its specificity, and can effectively be consigned to oblivion. A similar notion must have surely motivated the reciter of text 32 who declares that "their souls have just sunk over there, deep, far away, never to reappear!"

Invocation

To "awaken" the power-laden, but dormant, pantheon of cosmological forces Cherokee shamans often begin the recital of their prayers with an abrupt expletive such as *Gha!* This vacuous but attention-getting word device has been variously translated as 'Now!' 'Attention!' or 'Hear this!'

According to Olbrechts, in the second phase of the invocation shamans extol "the spirit's name, sometimes his color; the place where he has his abode" (Mooney and Olbrechts 1932, 159). A typical case is found in the divinatory spell, text 2, in which the creator is solemnly addressed as

tsane:hlanv́:hi ('you provider') *galv́la?di* ('above')
tsa:hlidho:hi:sdi ('resting place, your').

One might view this procedure as a complimentary "focusing" action, akin to the prefatory identity tag. By specifying the spirit by name, by its color trait, or by its celestial location, shamans literally scan the cosmos and select that spiritual entity which is most knowledgeable and skilled in affecting cures for their clients.

Having stirred the slumbering cosmos, Cherokee shamans move speedily to unruffle any ill will caused by their unwelcome interjections. As in lines two and three of text 2, reciters quickly placate the forces of nature by patronizing them with a litany of their supreme powers: "The one who foresees everywhere, you overlook nothing!" In the purification text 31, reciters demonstrate their reverence for the life-sustaining spirit of the water, Long Person, by proclaiming: "There is nothing that can overpower you!"

Another much vaunted phrase is *hida:we:hiyu*, which one might translate as 'You Great Wizard.' The reciter confers this exalted title upon the four various spirits who have been invoked in purification text 32.

These ingratiating phrases should not be perceived as just coy expressions of flattery. Rather, they serve as the necessary prerequisite to personal empowerment. To accomplish some supernatural act (which represents a temporary subversion of the natural order) permission must be sought and one's authority must be augmented from the cosmos. The human agency is powerless to manifest magic, even of the most innocuous sort, without direct guidance and aid from the governing pantheon of Cherokee spirits and deities.

Self-Affirmation

Self-aggrandizement, logically, finds its most frequent expression in love incantations, particularly those of the *ado:du:hiso ͻdi:yi* ('to rebeautify oneself') type. In the refrains of such love charms one often encounters such self-affirmative statements as "Now! I am as beautiful as ———." Here, reciters are ardently driven to compare their physical attributes to a range of avian spirits, chief among which are the radiant mythological *Tsugv:tsala:la* and the legendary roc-like bird, Dhla:nuwa.

In the present collection of magical formulae the reciter of text 25 personifies himself as an avatar of death, by proclaiming: "I am the Black Owl of Night!" By verbally assuming the form of this necrotic bird of prey sorcerers celebrate their exalted state as transmogrified bearers of supernatural force. Viewed from this perspective, one begins to understand these proclamations not as prideful boasts but as ritualistic exercises to strengthen the magic of practitioners.

Actualization

Having been granted supernatural powers to induce change, reciters then express their ritualistic intent by employing one of a myriad of verb phrases upon the object of their desires. Because the Cherokee language contains an astonishing number of verb forms (estimated by one author at one hundred thousand), it is logical that here, in the body of the text, ritual specialists would "show off" their lexiconic skill by employing diverse combinations of those verb phrases that they particularly relished.

In text 30, one such pyrotechnical display of verbal alchemy is cunningly calculated to overpower and to annihilate threats from malevolent forces. Addressing each deity in seriatim, the reciter weaves together a progressively violent set of directives: "You have just brought his heart down! . . . You have just leaped upon it! . . . You have just come to wrap around it!"

Time-Conflation

One of the key transformational statements in the Cherokee incantations presented here uses the curious verb suffix, -iga-('the subject has just come [to do something]'). Mooney was the first ethnolinguist to recognize the shamanistic insistence upon this peculiar verb form although he was at a loss to explain fully its ritual significance (Mooney 1891, 344).

Throughout this collection of spells one can readily observe the awkward coupling of this verb suffix with active infinitives to create such telling phrases as "You have just come to untie it," or "You have just come to wrap around it" (text 30), or "You have just come to strike it" (text 12). Other variants appear throughout as well: "He has just come to chop it up" (text 21); "You have just come to hear (text 22); and "you have just come to mourn" (text 23).

It has been observed that this -iga- suffix signifies that "at the time of speaking the action has just been performed" (Kilpatrick and Kilpatrick 1968, 67). Thus, it follows that this -iga- suffix serves a primary function in these ritualistic texts as a time-conflating device.

To foreshorten time "the present" (e.g., what is real, immediate, and tangible at this moment) must somehow be surrendered or bypassed. A future of remote and abstract possibilities must be telescoped into a circumvented "now" with such speed and authority that the discerning mind cannot challenge this transition and instead recognizes this change as only part of a natural succession of events.

To illustrate this dynamic consider the phrase "I have just come to draw away your soul." Whereas, the phrase, "I have come to draw away your soul," would simply announce one's intention, the shamanistic insertion of the adverb *just* dramatizes the fact that this ritualistic moment is now being actualized by the speaker's presence.

Just is a qualifying adverb that specifies the immediacy of one's actions in the context of time (e.g., "I have just been there" or "I have just been told"). By declaring their intention (e.g., to draw away the victim's soul) as a semi-completed temporal action reciters reinforce the illusion that metamorphosis has actually set in, that reality has already ("just now") been transcended.

Sometimes, another adverbial modifier, *u:sinu:liyu* ('quickly, very'), is added into such a phrase: "Very quickly I have just come to take away your soul!" This compounding of adverbial modifiers similarly co-opts time, accelerates the foregone ritual action (e.g., taking the soul), and, thus, renders it a fait accompli.

Synthesis

To effect traumatic physical or psychological change magicians occasionally resort to merging their powers with that of a supernatural entity. Usually, this process is achieved in the invocation section of the incantation by enlisting the sympathy of the natural force with flattering and ingratiating language as discussed earlier.

In text 19, however, whose purpose is to render the sorcerer invisible to enemies, reciters conjoin their skills of camouflage with that of their supernatural sponsor, the Black Mole. Thus, the reciter is free to announce, "You and I are dressed up in earth as One!"

In love magic such as the *age:hyv:ugv:wahli* ('women, for the purpose of') formulae, the desired outcome is to achieve physical or emotional synthesis with one's beloved. To accomplish this goal one usually employs transitory procedures to "remake" or "rebeautify" one's psyche. This ardent wish for some final unification often finds expression in such languid poetical phrases as "Your soul and mine will ever be inside of each other. Your flesh and mine will become one for as long as Time endures" (Kilpatrick and Kilpatrick 1965, 105).

Negative Reinforcement

The process of altering and influencing the thoughts and behavior of others requires reciters to strengthen their spells (and, conversely, weaken their prey) by expelling a series of negative declarations. In the realm of the magic spells presented here negative reinforcement usually takes the form of such hypnotically suggestive phrases as "those who think evil of me, you will never know it!" (text 17). Text 30a, transcribed by my late mother and labeled "This One is very difficult" exhibits another rich example: "The path will be lost forever, never to return!"

In purification text 31, the patient's desire to be restored to full health is underscored by the psychological imperative: "Something [evil] will never happen!" A similar hope permeates the phrase in text 32: "the intruder [illness] will never come again in their midst!"

Buttressing Devices

Embedded within each *i:gawé:sdi* text are carefully prescribed "buttressing" devices used to consolidate the power of the spell. The most vital of these elements is the standardized system of color symbolism employed by Cherokee traditionalists to induce psychological states in the patients/victims.

The color black, *gv:hnáge*, is often associated with the most extreme forms of physical illness or with death itself. The funereal atmosphere surrounding black is aptly illustrated in text 32, where the Evil Thinkers are consigned by the potency of the purification spell to repose forever in "black boxes" (coffins). In a similar vein in text 30, the Wicked Ones are condemned by the power of the conjuror's curse to suffer from the dreaded illness, "the very Black Evil."

The yellow hue, *dalo:ni*, connotes a sinister or malady-ridden condition. In text 16, the Yellow Man is invoked by the reciter of the spell to eat the souls of the Evil Thinkers.

Blue is most often associated with that peculiar Cherokeean melancholic state of love sickness, or uneasiness, known as *uhí:soʔdí*. In text 15, "To Placate the Angry" a myriad of consoling spirits (red, blue, black, and brown) are commanded to project this depressive state upon the harbinger of ill will: "The Blue he has found it!"

Red is a metaphorical color that, in the Cherokee ethos, connotes victory or good fortune. If a conjuror, himself, is threatened by the evil machinations of another wizard, then immediate protection must be sought. The most effective countermeasure, the most frequently mentioned defensive posture in the Cherokee realm of arcane, is to "attire" one's soul in this metaphysical color because it represents, to the Cherokee psyche, an inviolate state of well-being.

In text 28a, the magician attires those revered guardian spirits of Thunder and the Great Panther in this triumphant shade so that they can dispatch his enemies. In the "Going to the Water" divinatory text 10b, the legendary serpent, the Red *Ugh(a)dhe:ni*, is invoked to aid the reciter through the perilous and unhealthy Yellow pathways of his life.

The ethereal color white is usually employed to connote a transcendental state of peaceful calm or bliss. Thus, "white pathways," with their connotations of peace and personal fulfillment, are the object of desire in text 21, just as the "white feet" alluded to in text 17, are a symbol of a tranquil and serene state of mind. In purification texts such as text 31, are frequent references to "white cloths" and "white walking sticks," which serve as life-restorative symbols.

Two ritualistic shades of purple and brown are usually invoked in conjunction with other colors. In text 12, the tobacco spirit (arrayed in all of its manifestations of brown, white, black, and red) is called upon to "strike" down the illness promulgated by witchcraft. The purification described in text 32, is, again, infinitely strengthened by the participation of a myriad of multicolored spirits (red, purple, white, and yellow).

There is no metaphysical explanation for the omission of the color green, *ítseyú:sdi* ('of the new kind'), in Cherokee semiology. One would imagine that green would be highly regarded for its life-renewing properties. Cherokee conjurors, however, tend to view this verdant hue as an impoverished tool for servicing magic, and it is, therefore, excluded from the ritualistic repertoire.

Adjunctives

Cherokee magical formulae occasionally are accompanied by directives that outline the physical actions that should be taken to enhance the spell. These instructions are usually called *igú:n(e)dhi* ('to do it, one').

If only purification rites are to be conducted, then sorcerors will seek to augment their words with the generative power of natural springs or the flowing water of streams. When divinatory rites are performed to foretell the future or to identify the source of witchcraft, however, the surface of the water must be still. If the situation warrants it, a special, extremely potent brand of tobacco such as *Nicotiana rustica* L., known to its initiates in its magically "remade" state as *tso:lagayú:li* ('tobacco, ancient'), will be used to enhance the results (cf. Wilbert 1993).

Equally important to the overall efficacy of these rituals is the timing of their performance. Usually, *idi:gawé:sdi* are delivered at daybreak so that the celebrant facing the sacred direction of the east can receive the strength and illumination from the rising sun. The more evil forms of sorcery are usually actualized in the waning light of dusk or at the supernatural juncture of midnight.

By far one of the most commonly employed mechanisms to reinforce the efficacy of the spell is the simple numerical repetition of text. The most sacrosanct numbers in the Cherokee lexicon are four and seven. Most *idi:gawé:sdi* are then repeated, either quadrivially or septivially, depending on the gravity of the circumstances.

Wordplay

Mooney and Olbrechts were the first ethnolinguists to describe in any detail the use of "ritualistic language" in Cherokee shamanistic texts (1932, 160–65). In their view the curious transformations of sentences and wholesale substitutions of words that occured frequently in the sacred formulae of the eastern Cherokee could be attributed to three primary causes: (1) the insertion of archaic words; (2) the incorporation of other Cherokee dialects (particularly from the western *otali*, or 'overhill', group of speakers); and (3) from the programmic need to manipulate vocables to "fill out" the meter of various song-chants (1932, 161).

Although I agree with my predecessor's initial assessment, my own exegesis of the ritualistic language employed by Cherokee conjurors suggests that there exist a number of other reasons for its employment. Ethnographers studying the ceremonial life of indigenous groups have long noted the phenomenon of speaking or chanting "meaningless words" during a ritual performance. Characteristic of the songs/spells that feature this highly contrived form of communication is that the garbled words or phrases are not only incomprehensible to the audience but also to the speaker as well.

In the New World one of the earliest accounts of this type of ritualistic language is Hernando Ruiz de Alarcon's *Tratado de las supersticiones de los Naturales de esta N.E.* (Coe and Whitaker 1982, 42–44). Written in 1629, Alarcon's attack on the heretical Nahuallatolli, or the "disguised language" of the Nahuatl sorcerers, remains a prime source on native religion in central Mexico.

Among North American Indians, numerous ethnohistorical accounts exist of native folk healers using incomprehensible sounds in their own languages. In his *Nouveaux Voyages aux Indes Occidentales* (written in 1768) M. Bossu declares: "The savages have much confidence in their medicine men. . . . the language which he speaks in these invocations has nothing in common with the language of the savages; it is only through a heated imagination that these charlatans have found the means of making it pass for a divine language" (cited in Swanton 1928, 616).

Stephen Riggs, the missionary who compiled *Dakota Grammar, Texts, and Ethnography* in 1893, was one of the first scholars to note the "sacred discourse" of the Plains Sioux. Describing the "revelations made from the spirit world" by the Sioux *Wicasa Wakan* ('sacred men'), Riggs declared: "It is, then, only natural, that their dreams and visions should be clothed in words, many of which the multitude do not understand" (cited in Powers 1986, 20).

Scanning the ethnographic literature of the nineteenth century, one finds sporadic references to the ritualistic insertion of meaningless words as a vital component of Native American ceremonies. Boyle in his 1898 study of Iroquoian ceremonies describes the energetic incorporation of nonsensical sounds into their song-chant repetoire ([1898] 1986, 153, 155). Fenton in his 1942 monograph observed a similar phenomenon in the Seneca Great Feather Dance and the Oneida tracker's boasting song (Fenton [1942], 1986, 13, 19–20).

Swanton, in his comprehensive study of Creek religion and medicine, recorded two folk remedies from his informant, Caley Procter. Although both of the formulae concerned the treatment of serious physiological disorders, (e.g., curtailing the shortness of breath and staunching the flow of blood of patients), none of the words in either song-text appeared to hold any discernible meaning in the Creek language (Swanton 1928, 656).

Historically, it was common in Cherokee public ceremonies for both folk healers and participants to speak "meaningless" words. In August 1803 Moravian missionaries were treated to a Cherokee dance performance held at Estanelly Town House, Georgia. The white missionaries observed that the male drummers kept time for the ring of dancers by shaking "calabashes filled with small pebbles" and singing in accompaniment. They also perceived that "none of the words of these songs could be clearly recognized except *Hanji, Hanjo, hanani, johani*, which occured again and again. Brother Steiner asked what the song was supposed to mean. But everybody, even those who understand the language very well assured him that they could make nothing of it" (De Baillou 1961, 97).

Speck and Broom's study on Cherokee dance offers a plausible clue about why the audience was so puzzled by these unfamiliar sounds. They explain that historically during certain ceremonies, notably the Booger Dance (an Iroquoian vestige), the masked celebrants "pretend to speak other languages than Cherokee" ([1951] 1983, 28). Although the public exhibition witnessed by the Moravians was a different rite, one which celebrated harvests and fertility; nevertheless, it is possible that the ritualistic language spoken on this occasion was another inspired contrivance.

In another noteworthy early ethnohistorical account of Cherokee ceremonies Sarah Tuttle penned her observations of a Cherokee rain-making ceremony. She noted in 1823 that during the long period of fasting, which accompanies the rite, the conjurer "utters words incomprehensible to all but a few who have been instructed with the design of following the same practices" (Speck and Broom [1951] 1983, 9).

The general unfamiliarity with the words among the Cherokee audience in this case is not surprising. As Mooney and Olbrechts have observed, "The average member of the tribe may know four or five formulas but even then he usually knows fragmentary portions of them, as the ritual meaning of many words is unknown to him" (1932, 146–47).

Although the nature of the ritualistic language in public ceremonies might very well be the product of a lively imagination and the revelry of the moment, the same cannot be said for the employment of "meaningless" words in the shamanistic texts. Here, "the jealous care with which this material has been conserved and the judgement and the discrimination used when handing it down . . ." make it evident that the Cherokee folk healer consciously applied ritualistic language for a perceived effect (Mooney and Olbrechts 1932, 163).

Clearly, one motivation for Cherokee conjurors to use a strange set of vocalizations is that it represents, in their minds, sounds that are closely associated with certain spiritual entities. In texts 32 and 33, *ohanadu* and *hinadu* are symbolic sounds of the life-sustaining deity, Thunder, rendered as onomatopoeia.

Another possible motivation can be discerned by noting how the reciter of text 33 suddenly punctuates the spell by calling out the enigmatic word, *wahya* ('wolf'). Why? The most logical reason for this sudden choice is that the conjuror, attuned to Cherokee folklore, knew that members of the Wolf clan were endowed with special occult gifts and sought talismanic power from this guardian spirit.

Howard and Lena, in their study of the Oklahoma Seminole traditions, record a similar folkloric derivation behind the recitation of a string of "meaningless" syllables: *waku waku he wall yani yo*. In this case the authors note that the Muskogean word *waku* "refers to the blue crane *wakulakko*, who supposedly taught the songs to the ancestors of the Creeks and Seminoles" (Howard and Lena 1984, 70).

Other Cherokee scholars have speculated that some of the "meaningless" words in these magical texts function as ritualistic contractions (e.g., *woduhi* = *uwo:du:hiyu* ('very beautiful, it') (Kilpatrick and Kilpatrick 1967b, 106). Although no clear examples can be drawn from the present collection (text 24 might qualify), nevertheless, a few published specimens appear to support this thesis (Kilpatrick and Kilpatrick 1965, 102; Kilpatrick and Kilpatrick 1970, 120).

Euphemisms

The act of conjuring (particularly when it victimizes an individual) is considered unharmonious with the social ideals of Cherokee communities in which cooperation and consensus is the norm (see Gilbert 1943). Thus, one of the most utilitarian methods shamans use to mask their intentions is to employ euphemisms either in their private conversations or when they commit their formulae to paper.

In the 1960s, when the present collection was amassed, Cherokee conjurors in northeastern Oklahoma commonly used the phrase "to work" to characterize their esoteric practices. Among the eastern band a contrived phrase of similar meaning, "let us sit down together," is recorded by Mooney in his 1891 study.

Among the most venomous of the Cherokee formulae are those known under the rubric of *di:dagale:n(v)dho²di:yi* ('to separate them with, one'). This genre of magic is usually employed by a conjuror to break up love matches and to dispatch unwanted suitors. In certain cases, however, the shaman will foment the actual taking of a human life through the recitation of these formulae. Because of its highly potent nature, Cherokee conjurors often label their separation formulae with the innocuous phrase "to bring low."

Ritualisms

The use of ritualisms, first identified by Mooney and Olbrechts in their studies of supernaturalism among the eastern Cherokee, find close parallels in the western Cherokee material. Most often, practitioners of magic invoke ancient deities or mythological realms by contrived names known only to other cognoscenti. *Yv:wi Gana:hídv* ('Long Person') is an example of a formulistic term for a life-sustaining aquatic spirit that most often finds expression in "Going to the Water" purification rites such as those described in texts 31–33.

Mythological realms associated with the four cardinal directions are sometimes given formulistic appellations as well. In text 15, the mythological coordinate of the north remains the same as in conversational Cherokee, *uhyv́:dla:yi* ('cold place'). Its corresponding southern point (*ugá:no:wa* ['warm'] in ordinary Cherokee parlance), however, is celebrated by its ritualistic name, *wa:hela* ('where the eagle flies').

Mooney (1891, 377) records the corruptive form, *wa:hila*, as the eastern Cherokee nomenclature for the south. Upon reflection, this term appears to be a borrowing from the Creek designation for the south, *Wahá la* (cf. Speck 1964, 131).

Attenuation

A common device used to heighten the "sacred discourse" of the Oglala Sioux is attenuation, (the selected abbreviation of certain words), (cf. Powers 1986). Cherokee ritual specialists also employ this form of word play in their texts. These conscious ritualistic manipulations become quite apparent when one examines the various texts associated with the folk healer Uwe:da:sadhi Sa:wali.

In text 12, the literary device of aphesis (the omission of a prefix) can easily be observed. Thus, instead of the conventional word, *utsihna:wagwo* ('relief'), the author has substituted the abortive form, *tsihna:wagwo*.

Occasionally, the shaman will leave out the penultimate syllable in a word. This syncopic action can be observed in text 27 where the contracted form, *ghv:dhi* ('to use it, one'), was used in place of the ordinary spelling, *ghvdhó:dhi*.

Finally, in the unpublished Uwe:da:sadhi material apocopic changes (omission of the final suffix) are also employed to strengthen the spell. As a result, the curiously shortened form *ahnu:wo* ('cloth') appears in place of the traditionally elongated word *ahnuwo:gi*.

Archaisms

One of the more perplexing linguistic phenomena confronting a translator of this magical genre is the wholesale substitution of modern words for obsolete or long-forgotten terms. Cherokee magical practitioners, particularly those of twentieth-century vintage, regard archaisms as inherently powerful vehicles and constantly employ them in their spells despite the fact that often such words are no longer understandable even to the initiated.

The archaisms that appear in the present collection are derived from the same turn-of-the century source, Uwe:da:sadhi Sa:wali, and are to be understood, in my opinion, as references to celestial deities of unknown antiquity. The ancient entity Qwatloya is invoked for protection in text 19. Another possible archaic name is hiyidlaquv, which is encountered in the "Lower the Soul," text 30. In both cases my informants could offer no information about the meaning of these curious personal names or their possible mythological significance.

My late parents referred to a kind of index used by various Cherokee traditionalists to decode these mysterious words (Kilpatrick and Kilpatrick 1967b, 190). This rudimentary dictionary, which enables the contemporary shaman to make sense of these ancient expressions, is known in English as "to follow with the eye, one." Because I have no personal knowledge about such a source, the publication of a single "to follow with the eye, one," manuscript would be of considerable importance to future translators of Cherokee esoterica.

Loanwords

One of the most curious changes wrought by the twentieth century was the dual identity that most Cherokee medicine men came to assume. A surprising number of Cherokee ritual specialists, whose texts are featured here, professed Christianity during their lifetimes and took an active interest in their local churches. Many of these folk healers held titles as ordained ministers; others served as elders or deacons. These traditionalists seemed to make little distinction between their involvement with esoteric forms of enchantment and their participation in the worship of the Holy Trinity. Indeed, it appears that they were quite comfortable practicing both forms of native and western religion. As a result, many of the authors featured here found added inspiration by infusing their magical texts with such Christian elements as "amen" and "in the name of the Father, Son, and Holy Ghost"!

Cherokee folk healers were also quick to borrow magical phrases or even concepts from other tribes, most notably from the Muskogean-speaking groups who migrated in the 1830s into the Cherokee-settled areas of Oklahoma. It is evident that the Cherokees accepted this influx of Creeks, Natchez, and Choctaws as fellow kin, for at the turn of the twentieth century, when tribal governments were dissolved, these Muskogean-speaking migrants were "enrolled and allotted as Cherokees" (Kilpatrick and Kilpatrick 1967a, 29).

Most of these Muskogean people (along with their customs and beliefs) were eventually absorbed into the framework of Cherokee life through intermarriage, and some of them became active in the nativistic Keetoowah movements of the nineteenth century (Kilpatrick and Kilpatrick 1967a). Even today, a number of Muskogean speaking enclaves exist in northeastern Oklahoma. Some of the most prominent

Creek communities bordering the Cherokee territory are Sand Springs, located two miles south of Braggs; Beaver, located south of Bunch; and Vian Creek (aka "Eveningshade"), which is located north of the town of Vian.

In addition, an important community of mixed Creek-Natchez Indians at Cedar Springs is located between the town of Gore and the lower end of Lake Tenkiller in Sequoyah County. Some of the residents of this community, known locally as "Natcheetown," are descendants of the original Natchez band that was decimated by the French in 1729 and eventually migrated west with the Cherokee on the Trail of Tears in 1838–39.

The Natchez were highly regarded by the Cherokee "as a race of wizards and conjurers" (Swanton 1911, 255–56), whereas the Creek were equally esteemed for their magical abilities to put victims to sleep (Kilpatrick and Kilpatrick 1967b, 63). The Choctaws, some of whom settled near the town of Eufala in nearby McIntosh County, were a bit less welcome, especially those Choctaw who hailed from Mississippi, because they were "notorious as witches" (Tse:gi Ganv:hnawó:i field notes n.d.).

Viewed in this light, the magical traditions of the western Cherokee cannot be considered a "pure" ethnic expression. Rather, this corpus of texts reflects an amalgamation of diverse cultural influences that were introduced over time.

The Cherokee term for buzzard, *suli*, is unquestionably a Muskogean borrowing. (For its use among the Seminoles see Howard and Lena 1984, 167; its use among the Creeks is documented in Swanton 1928, 523.) In addition, the Cherokee word for the sacrosanct number seven, *ga:hligwo:gi*, has long been believed to be of Muskogean origin (Lounsbury 1961, 15).

Most prominently, Muskogean loanwords appear in Cherokee hunting and fishing spells in which the exotic nature of the incorporated foreign term is thought to empower the spell (cf. Kilpatrick and Kilpatrick 1967a). In the present collection, however, the most conspicuous example occurs in divinatory text 6.

Here, the female conjuror uses a divining crystal, known in Cherokee as *ulv:sadv* ('transparent') and invokes three enigmatic names to oversee the ceremony: Tsani, Megi, and Tasi (an unusual occurence in Cherokee *idi:gawé:sdi*). My own informants were mystified by this arrangement and could offer no logical explanation for these personal names.

The telling word here is *Tasi*, however, which, according to one source, is a Creek term for 'bluejay' (Speck 1964, 131). Mindful that the use of a divining crystal, the *sapiya* or *sabia*, is a well-known feature of the Muskogean magical traditions, the specter of foreign influence seems quite plausible here (for the use of the *sapiya* among the Creek see Swanton 1928, 498–501; among the Oklahoma Seminole see Howard and Lena 1984, 88, 91).

Dialectic Variation

One of the enduring failings of the Sequoyah syllabary is that it never developed a system for marking phonetic intonations. This is a critical omission for Cherokee is a highly inflective language in which even a minute change in the emphasis of a word can alter its meaning entirely. For example, when transcribing the Sequoyan script, one encounters words such as *hadina*, which, according to where the accent is placed, can exhibit myriad diverse meanings: *hadía* ('say, it'), or *haʔdí:na* ('ha, then'), or even *hadi:na* ('not'). In conversational Cherokee there is no confusion because speakers simply modulate their voices to convey the exact meaning intended.

Moreover, when transcribing the present set of texts, it was often difficult to tell whether a particular writer had committed an orthographic error or whether a case of errant spelling was simply the result of dialectal variation. For example, in text 2, Jackson Standingdeer, a medicine man from the Cherokee community of Gwagwo:hi, near the town of Barber, Oklahoma, records the conjunction *ali* ('and') instead of the more correct, *ale*. Does this represent a mistake by Standingdeer, or does it represent a convention of the *atsi:gvhnáge:sdhv:yi* ('black cedar place') dialect spoken in eastern Cherokee County during his life?

No thorough linguistic investigation has been conducted into the range of dialects spoken in northeastern Oklahoma. Although historically it is known that three regional dialects existed among the eastern Cherokees, there is intriguing ethnohistorical evidence, largely extracted from the letters of Moravian missionaries, that even during the early nineteenth century Cherokees living in Georgia and North Carolina spoke dialects "so totally different from each other that they sound[ed] like different languages" (McLoughlin 1984, 63).

The schematic of northeastern Oklahoma (map 2) extracted from my late father's notes represents a simplified division of the five major dialects known to have been spoken among the seventy-four Cherokee communities recorded in Albert Wahrhaftig's 1965 sociological survey.

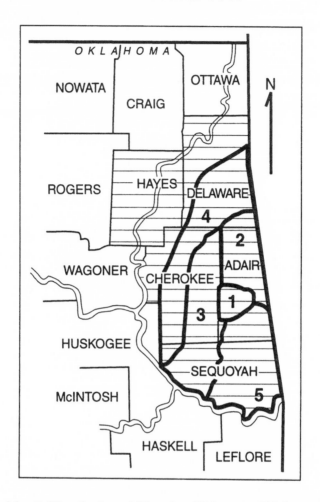

Map 2. Distribution of Cherokee Dialects in Oklahoma
1 = "Echota" 2 = "Thread" 3 = "Black Cedar" 4 = "Bluejay" 5 = "Cherry Tree"

Regarding the present collection of texts, it is known that both medicine men, Uwe:da:sadhi Sa:wali (1889–1936) and Siquinid (1911–1977) (who was of mixed Creek-Natchez and Cherokee heritage) hailed from eastern Cherokee County. Therefore, it can be assumed that they were conversant in a dialect known as *atsi:gvhnáge:sdhv:yi* ('black cedar place'), which is spoken in the native communities of Welling, Sugar Mountain, and Barber.

The majority of the other Cherokee authors in this collection (Green

Waterdown, Dlanus Toyanisi, Egi [1903–1953], and Uwo:digé Gigagé:i), lived in the southern portion of neighboring Adair County. Here, the principal Cherokee dialect spoken in the communities of Cherry Tree, Eunch, Salem, and Stilwell would be *gidhayo:hi* ('cherry tree place').

There is some manuscriptal evidence that the conjuror, Egi (1903–1953), lived near the town of Westville, in northern Adair County. Therefore, it is probable that he spoke the dialect of the local Cherokee communities of Christie and Old Green, which is known as *asdi:yi* ('thread place').

My late father recorded at least two other distinct Cherokee dialects spoken in the various Cherokee enclaves in northeastern Oklahoma. The first is *dlayigo:hi* ('black-jay place'), spoken in western Cherokee County around the communities of Hulbert and Fourteen Mile Creek and extending north into southern Delaware County, embracing the communities of Bull Hollow and Jay.

The final known variant of the Oklahoma Cherokee language is *it-sodi:yi* ('Echota place'). This specialized dialect was spoken by my own mother, who grew up in the Cherokee community of Echota, which is located west of the town of Stilwell, in Adair County.

"Tell Me the Way It Is"

Cherokee Divinatory Spells

Augury is an ancient art that has been viewed as a powerful tool of psychological resolution. By adumbrating future events the diviner can motivate individuals or groups to make significant life decisions in the face of unseen consequences.

Because of this, divination has been referred to as one of "the most important institutions of the primitive world" because it intercedes "in cases of illness and death . . . in the corroboration of a marriage choice and in individual or collective moves involving some change in social alignments, or, perhaps, economic condition; and in situations of loss, calamity, or unresolved conflict, whether on a personal or a much larger scale" (Park [1963] 1972, 386, 382).

Prognostication forms a salient part of the Cherokee medicomagical tradition. The motivations behind these activities have been aptly described elsewhere: "The Cherokees divine, and divine often, not to learn what the future is going to be, but to find out how the component parts of the present stand in relationship to each other. Nothing is preordained. The future will be pretty much what man requests the Provider to provide" (Kilpatrick and Kilpatrick 1967b, 86).

It is difficult to generalize about the nature of Cherokee divination rites primarily because it seems to be a singularly eclectic activity. Although certain fundamentals of the craft are recognized, Cherokees give wide latitude to interpreting their prophesies.

It might be fair to say that most Cherokees do not subscribe to self-imposed revelatory systems such as the *hanblečeya* tradition of the plains Sioux wherein divine guidance is gained through the rigorous oracle of the "vision quest." To the Cherokee mind if one wants to "know something" about the future, one can either "examine" certain natural signs, objects, or consult an appropriate authority.

Judging from colonial documents, Cherokee diviners seem to have held exalted status among their people: "They're strongly affected with dreams and run to their conjurers for an explanation, they likewise depend on their conjurers to foretell to them what success they'll have in Hunting and all their concerns" (letter from William Fyffe to Brother John February 1, 1761, cited in Woodward 1963, 42).

After the social upheavals of the nineteenth century, the old tribal customs of the Cherokee Nation withered under the stern gaze of the missionary. As a result, the role of diviners declined. They no longer prognosticated for the collective welfare of the people but worked as a type of private therapist who, for a fee, would service a client anxious about the future.

Traditionally, folk healers have two primary functions: diagnosis and treatment. Using their analytical skills, tempered by divine guidance, folk healers must discern from a myriad of possibilities the cause of their clients' sickness. Is it the result of witchcraft? or Is there some "natural" explanation? Is this sickness fatal or curable?

Having assessed the situation, folk healers then must decide what sort of treatment should be used. Is the folk healer even qualified to treat this disease? or Should the patient be referred to someone more experienced or better equipped to deal with this contingency?

Although there are some ritual formalities and procedures in divination that must be carefully followed, what ultimately ensures a positive and exacting "reading," according to my sources, is a humble attitude on the part of the supplicant. This is especially true in cases where the patient is suffering from some unknown pathogenic disease. "It is not so important for him to specifically diagnose the patient's disease. God will tell him what medicine to use. He may never know what the disease precisely is, but he will know the right medicine" (Tse:gi Ganv:hnawó:i field notes n.d.).

It is evident from this present set of texts that Cherokee diviners employed an astounding array of diagnostic tools in their practices. As impressive as this arsenal of objects is, Cherokees used a number of other material substances for prognostication that deserve mention.

Impending changes in the weather could usually be detected by studying the movements of a "rain" lizard or by noticing the location of a wasp's nest. According to folk wisdom, the number of red ant hills one encounters on a walk is a barometer of worsening conditions, such as oncoming storms (Tse:gi Ganv:hnawó:i field notes n.d.).

One can also presage unseen alterations in human lives by a variety of methods: by studying the placenta of a couple's latest child, diviners can forecast whether the parents will be further blessed in the future, or, if conditions are right, diviners can estimate the mortality of clients by counting the number of falling stars they see (Tse:gi Ganv:hnawó:i field notes n.d.).

In dire matters of health Cherokee diviners sometimes used human vomit as a source of revelation. Positioning their patients at the brink of a flowing stream, diviners administered an emetic. They then studied the patient's discharge in the water. If the vomit sank, the individual's condition was terminal; if the vomit stayed afloat, then the patient would eventually regain his or her health (Olbrechts 1930, 550).

Text 2

Gha!	*tsane:hlanv́:hi*	*galv́la?dí*
Listen!	you provider	above

tsa:hlidho:hi:sdi
resting place, your

nigv:nadv́:[na]	*higo:lodi:sgi*
everywhere	the one who foresees

gohú:sdi	*tsadehli:do:hi*	*nige:sv́:na*
something	overlook, you	being, not

ale	*hna:gwo*	*doyu:gh(o)dv*	*ditsa:notsa*
and	then	the good	it tells

tsadi	*tsadv:hnv́:hi*
you say	stated you

Free Translation

Listen! You Provider! You who reside above!
The One Who foresees everywhere!
You overlook nothing!
And you have stated that you tell the Truth!

Commentary

This text and its companion that follows were authored by the same individual, Jackson Standingdeer, a Cherokee medicine nan, who also served as a Baptist minister at the Sycamore Tree Church near Barber, Oklahoma, during the 1940s. The bound ledger book that contained these formulae was found buried in a glass fruit jar in a tree stump in 1964. The texts reproduced here date approximately from 1943 to 1946.

The exact method of divination is not specified here nor in the following text. It is possible that reciters are supposed to place their trust in the reciprocal relationship that exists between "the one who provides" and their earthly charges.

Text 3

Gha!   *i:gagadí*
Listen!   Holy Spirit

Gha!   *hna:gwo*   *agwane:hlanv́:hi*
Listen!   now!   the one who provides

i:gagadí   *asgwa:niyedv*
Holy spirit   astonishing it is

[de]gv́:yadhv: dhani:gá
I have come to question you

ugadv:svdv   *agwadhv:svli:ga*
the right thing   I have come to long for it

yv:wi   *u:nahl(i)sdéhlvdo'dí*
people   to help you with, it

tsadv:hnv́:hi   *na:gwo*
stated you   then

[de]gv́:yadhv'dhani:ga
I have just come to question you

Free Translation

Listen, Holy Spirit
Listen! Now! The One Who Provides
Holy Spirit! Astonishing it is!
I have just come to question You!
I have come to long for the Right Thing.
You stated that you would help the People.
Then I have come to question You!

Commentary

According to one of my informants, the word *i:gagadí* is the supreme ritualism for the concept of Morgenrote and connotes daybreak, or 'the light that breaks at dawn and dispells the darkness.' Since the Christianization of the Cherokee, the word has been taken to signify the Holy Spirit.

Text 4 "To Divine with Rock or Lead"

Caption

gohú:sdi   *agoliyé:svdi*
something   to examine it, one

Spell

tsane:hlanv́:hi
provider, you

gohú:sdi   *nitsa:ganelvna*
something   the one who knows everything

e:lohi   *nigv:nadv́:[na]*   *higowadiha*   *duyu:gh(o)dv*
earth   everywhere   deliver   truth

hade:loho:sgi
one who foresees

na dvdá:sginohiseli   *tsiyudi ge:sv́:i*
now you remake it   the way it is [the right way]

Free Translation: "To Examine Something"

You Provider! The One who knows all.
Deliver the truth everywhere!
The One who Foresees
Now You Remake it the Right Way.

Commentary

This divinatory prayer was dictated to my late father by "a kindly traditionalist," the medicine man Uwo:digé Gigagé:i, on June 11, 1963. Always circumspect about their activities, Cherokee practitioners of magic
frequently use euphemisms such as "to read" or "to examine" to camouflage their attempts at divination.

No instructions were recorded during this session. Heavy, solid objects like stones, however, are usually held in the hand and rotated by
folk healers, who give a type of psychometric reading based on their
interpretations of the peculiar properties of the stone. This formula,
striking in its simplicity, bears some resemblance to a divinatory text
found in a medicine book belonging to my mother's great uncle, which
dates to the late nineteenth century:

Text 4a

You, everywhere upon Earth, the Provider,
I petition you:
Tell me what You know concerning this.

Text 5   "To Divine with the Lead"

Caption

gohú:sdi	*aga:dhv:di*	*ga:ni*
something	to look, one	lead

gv:dho:di	4	*iyuwa:judi*
to use, one	four	times

Spell

une:hlanv́:hi	*gahligwo:gi*
the provider	seven

i:yágalv:la[di:yá]	*tsa:hlidho:hi:sdv*
above, the [heavens]	to repose, you

u:sinu:liyu	*hwigvyá:dvgoda*
quickly, very	I have just come to let you know

ni:galv́:lohi	*di:tsa:hlido:hi:sdi*
there, on high	resting place, you

u:sinu:liyu	*sgwadvgo:hlani:ga*
quickly, very	you have just come to let me know

Free Translation

To examine something, one uses lead four times.

Provider, quickly, I have just come to let you know
from your resting place in the Seventh Heaven!
Very Quickly, You have just come to let me know
from your resting place on high!

Commentary

Because individual preferences abound, a variety of metal objects can be employed for divination: gold, silver, or lead. What ultimately matters is that the substance "comes from the ground" (Kilpatrick and Kilpatrick 1967b, 114).

Green Waterdown, the author of this text, left explicit instructions about the correct procedures to be followed here. A lead object is suspended from a string. Then it is swung from the hand, pendulumlike. As it rotates on the string, the diviner notes which cardinal direction it seems to favor. East is considered a "good" sign and is associated with a positive result.

Text 6 "To Use the Ulv:sadv"

tsani	*megi*	tasi
John [?]	[?]	bluejay

tsane:hlanv́:hi	*hna:gwo*
provider, you	now

gayadhvdv:hv ʔ:sgi	*agidhvdi:yi*
I will question you	to procure it

Free Translation

John [?] Megi [?] Bluejay!
You Provider!
Now! I will question you.
Procure the answer.

Commentary

This divinatory formula was dictated to my late parents by a medicine woman whose Cherokee name was Dutsili (?) Uné:gv (White), on July 25, 1966. An accompanying note, written in English, states that this is a *juwayoi* ('divining') *i:gawé:sdi* ('formula') copied from a book of hers.

The *Ulv:sadv* ('shone through, it') is a transparent quartz rock, which, according to legend, was extracted from the forehead of an extremely lethal mythological serpent, Ukten. The crystal allowed its owner to manifest supernatural powers to forecast the future (Mooney 1900, 297, 458–59; Olbrechts 1930, 549).

The use of a divining crystal, the *sapiya*, or *sabia*, is a well-known feature of the Muskogean magical traditions. There are scattered references to it in the ethnographic literature on the Creek (Swanton 1928, 498–501), and the Seminole (Howard and Lena 1984, 88–90).

According to Gilbert, the aboriginal Cherokee employed polygon-shaped pieces of crystalline quartz in their divinatory rituals, which they called "lights" (1943, 345). These glittering stones were cut to five separate sizes. "The largest was used in war divination; the next largest for feasts, purification, and divination concerning sickness; the next for hunting; the next for finding things lost or stolen; and the smallest for determining the time allotted for anyone to live" (345).

Instructions accompany this text. One puts the *ulv:sadv* into a dish of water. A square has been inscribed into the bottom of the dish, and the names of four Indian doctors have been drawn into each of the four corners of the square. As the water is removed from the dish, the crystal will float toward one of the corners, indicating its choice of a physician. If the crystal floats out of the assigned square, the patient will get well.

Besides these procedures, the crystal may become discolored or turn black, indicating that the patient's condition is terminal (cf. Olbrechts 1930, 549). Conversely, the client's image may appear to the diviner within the crystal, which is a hopeful sign of recovery.

This text remains something of an enigma. The possibility exists that the first three words that appear here are personal names (an unusual occurence in Cherokee *idi:gawé:sdi*). Tsani, after all, is the Cherokee derivative for the English name, Johnny. Tasi is a Creek term for 'blue-jay' (Speck 1964, 131). One might also hazard a guess that Megi is a Creek loan word or a Cherokee derivative for the name, Maggie (usually rendered as 'Negi'). My Cherokee informants could offer no logical explanation for this section.

Text 7

Caption

agoli[ye]:svdi   *gohú:sdi*
to examine   something

Spell

Gha!   *tsane:hlanv́:hi*
Listen!   provider, you

hna:gwo   *yv:gi tsu:[na]sdi*
now   needle pin

degv́:yadhv꜔dani:gá   *gohú:sdi*
I have just come to ask you   something

tlidehli:do:hi   *nige:sv́:na*
to keep a secret to he, she, it   never

hna:gwo	*na:gwu*	*duyu:ghodv:i*	*dv:sgíhno:ne:lí*
now	then	truth	you will tell me

hino	*iyú:sdi*	*aguadu:lihá*	*agwátlogehisdi:i*
this	thing	I want to know	where I am going

Free Translation

Listen, You Provider
Now I have come to ask the One
who keeps no secrets with the Needle Pin
And You will Tell me the Truth
This Thing I want to know.

Commentary

This divinatory text bears the date of 1946 and was authored by Jackson Standingdeer. The accompanying ritual is timed to coincide with dawn and is usually conducted to evaluate the seriousness of a patient's affliction. In their deliberations Cherokee diviners sometimes use two pine needles or two metal sewing needles, which, when balanced on a middle finger, are set adrift one by one in a bowl of water. With practiced eyes diviners then study the movements of the needles floating in the water: "If the lefthand needle dives over . . . and touches its companion, a poor prognosis is obtained; if the sinistral needle strikes the dextral one, . . . only the most extraordinary efforts can save the patient. If, however, the needles keep their distance or float even further apart, the outlook is hopeful" (Kilpatrick and Kilpatrick 1967b, 116).

Text 8

nv:ya	*[a]diga:dodi*	*agadv:dodi*
stone	my father!	grandfather!
[spoken four times]		

gha!	*hna:gwo*	*da:sgihno:heseli*
Listen!	now	you will tell me

hna:gwo	*gvyá:dhú:dvni:gá*	*sqwane:hlanv́:hi*
now	I have just come to question you	provider, my

gadono	*u:sdi aneda:nv:dhéhlidoha*
what	what are they thinking

ha!	*yv:wi*	*ge:sv:i*
ha!	the people	it is

Free Translation

Stone! My Father! My Grandfather!
[spoken four times]
Listen! You will tell me now!
I have come to question you, My Provider!
What? What are they thinking?
Ha! The People it is!

Commentary

This divinatory spell, which dates to 1943, was also authored by Jackson Standingdeer. As in text 5, a stone is suspended upon a string, and its free-ranging movements are watched.

This type of formula is often used in cases of litigation when the client is anxious to discern what a jury is thinking (cf. Kilpatrick and Kilpatrick 1967b, 100–101). One occasionally finds natural forces (e.g., wind, rain) addressed in paternal terms as in this text (Kilpatrick and Kilpatrick 1967b, 33).

Text 9   "To Divine with the Stones"

Caption

gohú:sdi	*nv:ya*	*digv:dodi*
something	stone	to use

Spell

une:hlanv́:hi	*galv́la?di*	*tsa:hlido:hi:sdi*
provider	above	to rest, you

hna:gwo	*da:sgino:hiseli*
now	you will tell me

nu:sdv	*gada:nv:dhé:sgv:i*
what	I am thinking about

agwadu:lihá	*agwadé:logehisdi:i*	*duyu:ghodvi*
I want	to find out	the truth

Free Translation

Something to use a stone with.
Provider, Your resting place is Above.
Now, you will tell me
what I am thinking about.
I want to learn the truth.

Commentary

The author of this brief divinatory prayer was Joe Waterdown. According to the epigramic instructions that accompany the text: "Hold 2 small stones (size of acorns), one in one hand, one in other. Say 4 times. Then examine rocks. If one in right hand moves, good; converse, bad. Keep the stones. Do not throw away."

According to Cherokee folk belief, once divining stones are prayed over, they become temporarily imbued with magical powers. To reenergize that essence the stones must be "remade." To this author's knowledge the only known example of this magical rite is a text labeled "To Remake Divining Stones," which was transcribed into English for my father in 1965 by the Creek-Cherokee medicine man Siquanid:

Text 9a

Now! You Provider!
Ha! Now You who have made the Stones alive,
You have just come to raise me up.
I have just come to ask You things.
(Looking all about Him, He has just come to perform.)
Now! Listen! Your soul has just been pushed
against the middle of the Pathway where it divides!

According to the notes that accompany this text, the above incantation is recited four times over four small stones that have been placed on top of the water. The stones can then be used to "find out all things." The efficacy of the stones is strengthened if an individual conducts the ritual early in the morning. It is also observed that "one makes himself more of a wizard by washing his face first."

Text 10

Caption

| *tso:la* | *go:dhlv?di* | *ghilo* | *yí:galeha* |
| tobacco | to make it, one | someone | if conjuring you, they |

Spell

| *hadía* | *digwadó:idv́* |
| say, it | named, I |

×
[recites the patient's name]

| *ditlidóidv́* | × |
| named, clan, my | [recites the name of clan] |

| *ha? dí:na* | *Wajuli* |
| ha, then | Whippoorwill |

| *di:gh(a)dha* | *degv́:yelina* |
| eyes, they | I have just come to draw them out |

| *ha? dí:na* | *Ahwi* |
| ha, then | Deer |

| *di:gh(a)dha* | *degv́:yelina* |
| eyes, they | I have just come to draw them out |

| *ha?dí:na* | *Dhla:nuwa* |
| ha, then | Tsunuwa |

| *di:gh(a)dha* | *degv́:yelina* |
| eyes, they | I have just come to draw them out |

haʔdí:na	*Huhu*
ha, then	The Yellow Mockingbird

di:gh(a)dha	*degṹ:yelina*
eyes, they	I have just come to draw them out

Free Translation

To make tobacco if someone is conjuring you.

Ha, then I have just come to draw out eyes of the
Whippoorwill!
Ha, then I have just come to draw out the eyes of the
Deer!
Ha, then I have just come to draw out the eyes of the
Dhla:nuwa!
Ha, then I have just come to draw out the eyes of the
Yellow Mockingbird!

Commentary

The entity appealed to here is Dhla:nuwa (variously known as Sa:nuwa and Dlani:gwa), an enormous spirit bird of great antiquity said to exhibit a "hawklike mien" and to indulge in "man-eating proclivities" (see Kilpatrick and Kilpatrick 1965, 28 for bibliographic references about the appearance of this ferocious avian deity in Cherokee folklore and mythology). Huhu, or the Yellow Mockingbird (the yellow breasted chat, *Icteria virens virens*), appears with great frequency in Cherokee folklore and in magical incantations (for bibliographic references see Kilpatrick and Kilpatrick 1965, 22). This charming avian spirit figures prominently in love charms, protective formulae, and wealth-gaining spells. His appearance, here, in a divinatory text is unusual, but he often shares his company with Dhla:nuwa.

This divinatory text was found in the papers of a medicine woman, Dutsili (?) Uné:gv (White). It appears to be recited as a "Going to the Water" rite. The general methodology for divining at the brink of the stream is to cut off a blackjack oak branch, about two or three feet long, denude it of its leaves, and stir this stick counterclockwise in a flowing stream of water, creating a circle. One then observes what floats into this circle of water. Certain objects are thought to be indicative of a patient's prognosis: if a leaf or a crayfish floats into the circle's perimeter, then the patient's future is not hopeful. If, however, no object invades the circle and the water remains calm, then the patient's recovery is ensured.

The authoress also left a description of an alternative ritual. An individual digs a hole at the edge of the water in a proscribed counterclockwise fashion and then lets the water seep into the hole. One holds the stick in the middle of the water. Then this spell is recited four times while the movement of objects within the circle of water is studied. If a crayfish surfaces within this designated area, then it is a sign that the patient has been bewitched by an enemy. If a butterfly flitters into the circle, then the omen is favorable. To conclude the ritual one drinks water from the hole and washes one's face from the same source.

Tree limbs are considered the best vehicle for divining the cause of a patient's illness. If the folk healer, however, becomes afflicted, then other diagnostic measures must be taken. In this case, the folk healer, holding a gha:ni ('arrowhead'), would then recite a "Going to the Water" text similar to this one found in the papers of medicine man Green Waterdown:

Text 10a

Now! I have just come to You.
Ha! Ya! Right here is my name:
Ha! I have just come to ask You,
You whose name is Arrowhead.
I am asking You about many things.
Seven Clan Places!
All of you have been told nothing!

In a number of divinatory "Going to the Water" texts the principle psychometric instruments are beads held in the hand. The object of this type of text is usually to discern the nature of a patient's illness. The caption of one such text found in the papers of Uwe:da:sadhi Sa:wali indicates that one is "to bathe at night in the stream and to use white beads." Most "Going to the Water" texts invoke either the river spirit, Long Person, or the Supreme Being. This particular example is unusual because the deity addressed here is an enormous, poisonous serpent:

Text 10b

The Yellow Pathway lies before me.
Ha, then! Red Ugh(a)dhe:ni!
Ha! I just scraped along against
his tail,
you who walk about over there in
the Seven Clan Places.
All of you who Think the Important
one upon me are not to climb
over me.

The Yellow Pathway lies before me.
Ha, then! I am scraping along against
the Red Ugh(a)dhe:n(i)!
You Seven Clan Places began
what you have become.
I have just come to climb over
all of you over there.
Ha, then! I have just come to
have a confrontation with Knowledge!

Text 11 "To Divine with Spider Roots"

Gha! hi²a² hna:gwo dagú:yadhv:dv:hi tsane:hlanú:hi
Now! this now I will question you provider, you

ga²do u:sdí dunada:nv:dá:diyi duyu:ghodv:i
what that you know about the truth

hade:lohó:sgi
one who foresees

tsigi hna:gwo da:sgino:hiseli
it is now you will tell me.

nu:sdv unada:nv:da:i ge:sv:i
what how they feel it is

Free Translation

Now! I will question you, You Provider!
What you know about the Truth!
You will tell me, the one who Foresees
What are they feeling?

Commentary

To my knowledge this text represents the only recorded example of an antiquated divining rite that uses di:nada'ne:sg(i), or spider roots (botanical name unknown), to detect witchcraft. According to the instructions recorded by the Cherokee medicine man Uwe:da:sadhi Sa:wali, one uses two spider roots, each about 22 inches long, which are placed, side by side, in the palm of the hand. The text above is recited, and the reciter chews sassafras roots and then spits onto the outstretched hand. This whole procedure is repeated four times. After this, one examines the spider roots held in the palm: if the root on the right moves over and touches the one on the left, then no witchcraft has been invoked. If, however, the left root moves over and entwines itself with the right one, the patient has, indeed, been conjured, and remedial measures must be quickly taken. The utility of this formula is evident because its author states that it "can be done *anytime*."

Although the Cherokees place great faith in the infallibility of spider roots to detect witches, the Iroquois advocate the use of an aquatic plant known as Big Root, or Yellow Pond Lily (*Nuphar luteum variegatum*). Big Root and several other unnamed herbs are blended together and brewed as a tea, then served to a suspected evildoer. If the prime suspect reacts violently to the tea, one's worse fears are confirmed (Herrick 1983, 135–36).

"To Turn One Aside"

Cherokee Protective Charms

James Adair, in his *History of the American Indians*, recounts an episode in 1765 when he was visited by a Cherokee medicine man. Before entering Adair's abode, the "old physician looked in a frightful manner, from the southwest toward the north" and then engaged in a long series of guttural chants: "After his song, he stepped in. . . . He said . . . he could not do me a more kind service than to secure my house from the power of the evil spirits of the north, south, and west, . . . and, from witches, and wizards, who go about on dark nights, in the shape of bears, hogs, and wolves, to spoil people" (Adair [1775] 1930, 185).

Upon reflection, Adair's "old physician" was most probably reciting a *dida:gwohlv́:sdo:dí* ('To Turn One Aside') spell. Defensive in nature, these highly potent protective charms form a specialized branch from a larger tree of Cherokee esoteric formulae.

The complexity of a particular "To Turn One Aside" spell seems to depend, in part, on the gravity of the circumstances. The most common form of "To Turn One Aside" formulae are those used rather like St. Christopher medals to safeguard one's journey to a particular destination (see texts 20–21).

Another prominent use is to shield one during social gatherings when one is surrounded by unfamiliar people. As a rule, Cherokees treat all strangers with a high degree of reticence and caution. This is especially true if the stranger happens to be a fellow Cherokee. This circumspect social attitude has been eloquently described elsewhere:

> They are careful not to offend by the word or deed that might be misinterpreted as hostility; for there is the ever-present danger that the visitor might resort to witchcraft to avenge a fancied slight or insult. Silence,

not forced small talk, is the proper climate for solidifying social content; the jest is an embossed invitation to trouble (Kilpatrick and Kilpatrick 1967b, 139).

If one does commit a social faux paus and incurs the wrath of an individual, then it is best to initiate a type of spell that is known as *digvghé:hw(i)sdoˀdhí:yi* ('To Make Them Forget With'). This special incantation is designed, as in texts 15 and 17, to induce a state of psychological forgetfulness in a vengeful or spiteful individual.

Finally, the most crucial forms of "To Turn One Aside" formulae are recited to counteract the machinations of adversaries in life-threatening situations. A host of such dire occasions are recorded here when one must protect oneself from the psychic energies of the dead (text 18), mean-spirited entities known as *ane:li:sgi* ('those who think purposefully') (text 16), conjurors (texts 12–14), and various terrifying creatures of the night (texts 22 and 24).

Text 12 "For Something Done to Them"

Caption

nasgi:no	*tso:la*	*ghvdhoˀdi*	*osani*
this, and	tobacco	to use it	fine

ase	*na:sgi*	*iyú:sdi*	*geso:i*
perhaps	this	kind	it was

sa:gwo	*i:yu yi:gi*
one	at any time

diya:sgwada	*atsoda:sdi watsi:la*	*ganvliye:di*
when you finish	to blow saliva	to rub, one

gv:hnagé:i	*unehisdá:ne:hv́:i*	*na:sgi*
black	hurting, they	that

hiˀaˀ	*junu:sdi*	*tsotsi:gasiha*
this	root	"to point out three"[?]

udo:yu	*tsilv́:qwodi:yu*
truly	I like it, much

gohú:sdi	gegv:nelvhi		yi:gi
something	have been put in this condition		if it is

Spell

gha	sge:ʔ	tso:la	wodigé:i
now	listen	tobacco	brown, it

gv:dhani:ga
have just come to strike it

haʔdí:na	[u]tsihna:wagwo	nigvdísge:sdi
ha, then	relief	I will be saying

ya	tso:la	uné:gv	gv:dhani:ga
ye!	tobacco	white, it	have just come to strike it

ya	tso:la	gv:hnagé:i	gv:dhani:ga
ye!	tobacco	black, it	have just come to strike it

haʔdí:na	[u]tsihna:wagwo	nigvdí:sge:sdi
ha, then	relief	I will be saying

ya	tso:la	gigagé:i	gv:dhani:ga
ye!	tobacco	red, it	have just come to strike it

haʔdí:na	[u]tsihna:wagwo	nigvdí:sge:sdi
ha, then	relief	I will be saying

Free Translation

Perhaps this tobacco was the one that was fine to use at any time. When you finish [reciting the spell], one blows saliva and rubs it if they are hurting from the Black [an affliction]. This root, "to point out three" [botanical name unknown], I truly like it if someone has been put in this condition.

Now! Listen! The Brown Tobacco has just come to strike it!
    Ha, then! Relief, I will be saying!
Ya! The White Tobacco has just come to strike it!

Ha, then! Relief, I will be saying!
Ya! The Black Tobacco has just come to strike it!
 Ha, then! Relief, I will be saying!
Ya! The Red Tobacco has just come to strike it!
 Ha, then! Relief, I will be saying!

Commentary

This ritual, recorded in the Uwe:da:sadhi Sa:wali papers, is designed to counteract the effects of the victim who was conjured. The text is to be said only once while "remaking" tobacco during the course of one day. One is to blow four times (once for each stanza of the spell). The instructions are explicit about using store-bought chewing tobacoo as the main ingredient and not the special species of *Nicotiana rustica* L. or *tso:lagayú:li* ('ancient tobacco') used for most other ceremonies of great import.

The field notes of Frans Olbrechts record another counteractive remedy to witchcraft used by the North Carolina Cherokees. Here, when a patient "feels queer" (a telltale sign of being conjured), the individual is directed to drink a tea made of the bark of * adaˀ tsú:sihwá* ('the hollow wood'), or striped maple (*Acer pennsylvaniceum* L.), which has been strengthened with several other unidentified ingredients (Kilpatrick and Kilpatrick, "Eastern Cherokee Ethnobotany," n.d.).

Text 13 "For a Poultice"

Caption

ga:dhidv	i:gawé:sdi
missile	to say it, one

Spell

sgi:nvsidasdi	sgi:geyuhiyu	higa[yv]:li	gigagé: i
I am your servant	you love me	ancient, one	red, it

gvyo:sehi	tsali:sdayvdi
I say to you	something for you to feed yourself with

sgi:gaha	usv:hidv	agwadv:hisv	v́:dla
you own me	overnight	I long for it	not

gohú:sdi *yegv:giyalvgi*
something to stick on me

Free Translation

A missile incantation.

I am your servant! You love me!
Ancient Red One! You own me!
I say to you that this is your food
I do not want something to stick on me overnight.

Commentary

The *ga:dhidv* is a supernatural projectile shot through the air by a witch. Once it lodges in the victim's body, illness or death will occur. This brief text appeals to the powerful force of the Ancient One to circumvent this magical penetration. There are no instructions accompanying this text, which was recorded during the period 1940–41. It is attributed to Egi, a Cherokee medicine man who hailed from Adair County.

Cherokee medicinal remedies exist to counteract the evil effects of being "shot," which do not require the recitation of a magical incantation to ensure their efficacy. One of these folk remedies recommends that the patient use a red sassafras root about eight inches long taken from the eastern side of the tree. One extracts the outer bark, washes the root until it is very clean and then pulverizes it. The granulated sassafras is added to a crushed polk root, originally six inches long. Finally, one sprinkles in cornmeal and applies this poultice to the afflicted area overnight. To ensure the health of the patient the procedure should be repeated for four days (Tse:gi Ganv:hnawó:i field notes n.d.).

Text 14 "For a Poultice to Remove a Foreign Object Introduced by Sorcery"

gho:la *hísvga*
bone you stink!
[4 times]

Free Translation

Bone, You stink!
[4 times]

Commentary

This folk remedy was dictated to my late father by a medicine woman whose English name was Lizzie Swimmer on August 12, 1963. The procedure recommended here is to take a handful of *awun(nv)niyonv* 'horehound' (*Marrubium vulgare*) and put a small amount into a bag made of white cloth. To make the poultice the bag is then pounded until its contents become "slimy." Opening the bag, the practitioner then recites this formula, blows upon the substance, and spits upon it four times. Then the poultice is applied to the inflicted area of the patient and left overnight.

During the colonial period Cherokee folk healers used wild horehound as a poultice to draw out snakebites (Adair [1775] 1930, 247–48). No doubt, acknowledged here is the symbolic connection between the poisonous bite of a snake and the equally debilitating venom of the conjuror.

Text 15 "To Placate the Angry"

gha	*hi:sgaya*	*gigagé:i*
now	man, you	red, one

nv:do:gv:yi	*ditsa:hl(i)dho:hi:sdv*
sun-land	reposing place, your

hi:sgaya	*ditsa:gani*	*de:gaduno*	*galo:si:ga*
man, you	he eyes you	village	over here he just came to pass by

duda:nvdo?gihi	*nunv:istanvdv*
soul, his	without hitting

u:sinu:liyu	*udiniliga*
quickly, very	he has just brought it

wadvhi	*dudú:tlidi:degesdi*
he found it	he will be covered

gha!	*hi:sgaya*	*sa?gho:ni*
now	you man	blue

uhyṹ:dla:yi   *ditsa:hl(i)dho:hi:sdv*
cold land   to rest, you

hi:sgaya   *ditsa:gani*   *de:ganduno*   *galo:si:ga*
you man   he eyes   you village   over here he just
                                                  came to pass by

duda:nvdoʔgihi   *nunv:istanvdv*
soul, their   without hitting

u:sinu:liyu   *vdiniliga*
very quickly   he has just brought it

utsohladigwo   *di:nutli:dani:ga*
fumes   you have just covered it

saʔgho:ni   *wadvhi*   *dudṹ:tlidi:degesdi*
blue   he found it   he will be covered

gha   *hi:sgaya*   *gv:hnáge*
now   you man   black

wasv:hi   *ditsa:hl(i)dho:hi:sdv*
west?   to rest, you

hi:sgaya   *ditsa:gani*   *de:gaduno*   *galo:si:ga*
you man   he eyes you   village over   here he just came
                                                  to pass by

duda:nvdoʔgihi   *nuwa:vstanvdv*
soul, his/her   without moving it

u:sinu:liyu   *vdinigali*
very quickly   he has just brought it

utsoladigwo   *vdi:nutli:dani:ga*
fumes   you have just covered it

saʔgho:ni   *wadvhi*   *dudṹ:tlidí:degesdi*
blue   he found it   he will be covered

*gha*ʔ   *hi:sgaya*   *wodigé:i*
now   you man   brown, it

wahála   *ditsa:hl(i)dho:hi:sdv*
south   reposing-place, your

hi:sgaya   *ditsa:gani*   *de:gaduno*
you man   he eyes you   village

galo:si:ga
over here he just came to pass by

*duda:nvdo*ʔ*gihi*   *nuwa:vstanvdv*
soul, his   without moving it

u:sinu:liyu   *vdiniliga*
very quickly   he has just brought it

utsohladigwo   *vdi:nutli:dani:ga*
the fumes   you just covered it

*ha sa*ʔ*gho:ni*   *wadvhi*
ha blue   he found it

Free Translation

Now, You Red Man, you rest in the Sunland!
You Man, he eyes You. He has just passed by the village without hitting his soul. Very Quickly he has found it [the fumes] and brought it. He will be covered [with the fumes].

Now, You Blue Man, you rest in the Cold Land.
You Man, he eyes You. He has just passed by the village without hitting his soul. Very Quickly he has just brought the fumes. You have just covered it with fumes. The Blue he found it. He will be covered!

Now, You Black Man, you rest in the West!
You Man, he eyes you. He has just passed by the village without moving his soul. Very Quickly he has just brought the fumes. You have just covered it with the fumes. The Blue he has found it. He will be covered!

Now, You Brown Man, you rest in the South.
You Man, he eyes You. He has just passed by the village without moving his soul. Very Quickly he has just brought the fumes. You have just covered it with fumes. Ha! The Blue he has found it!

Commentary

The purpose of this text is to induce a psychological state of memory loss in an adversary who bears the client ill will. To achieve this goal a complex set of directives must be followed by the reciter, which usually involves symbolically "remaking" tobacco or engaging in a purification rite known as "Going to the Water" (see chap. 6).

One can observe in the text the delicate verbal juxtapositions that are employed by the reciter to remove anger from the offended party. First, the reciter invokes sympathetic spiritual forces from all four of the cardinal directions. It is noteworthy that these powers are addressed in counterclockwise fashion (e.g., east, north, west, and south) because this is a symbolic movement to "undo" evil.

Allied with these primal forces of nature and infused with transmutational power the reciter can now quickly transfigure the soul of the unhappy and vengeful person into a subliminal effigy of itself by covering it with a dense, lethargic smoke screen: "You have just covered it with fumes!" By doing this, the enflamed spirit of the offended party is not only dowsed with a calming emotional state but also his very memory becomes blurred.

To complete the spell the reciter crystallizes an abject state of despair and projects it upon the intended victim: "The Blue! He has found it!" By "filling up" the victim with a temporary, but heavy and depressive psychological mood the conjuror softens the aggressive nature of the grudge-holder. As a result, it is hoped that no retaliatory action will take place against either the conjuror or the client.

Text 16 "To Counteract Evil Thinkers"

Caption

digá:dhli:dhadi:sdí	gohú:sdi
to put them to sleep, one	something

ane:li:sgi   *dini:sdodi*
thinkers   to prevent

tso:la   *go:dhlvhiso?dhi*
tobacco   to remake, it

Spell

gha!   *sge?*   *a:sgaya*   *dalo:ni*
Now   listen   man,   yellow
                        he,

ha   *u:sinu:li*   *denatsaga:hlawi:sdani:gá*
ha   quickly   they have just come to live with you

ha   *dine*   *gvwadhú:hwidv*   *getsadla:hw(i)sdi:de:ge:sdí*
ha   then   everywhere   they will be living with you

u:yo? duda:n(v)di   *hna:gwo*   *dine diga:i*
evil mind, his/her   now   you that much

higa
eat it

a:sgaya   *sa?gho:ni*
man   blue

a:sgaya   *gv:hnagé:i*
man   black

a:sgaya   *dalonige:i*
man   yellow

ya!!   4 ×
ya!!   [four times]

Free Translation

To put to sleep something. To Prevent Thinkers.
Remake Tobacco.

Now! Listen! Yellow Man! Ha!
Quickly! They have just come to live with you!
Ha, then! They will be living with you everywhere!
Now, You Eat Their Evil Minds!
Blue Man! Black Man! Yellow Man! Ya!
[The spell is to be recited four times]

Commentary

"Thinkers" are those individuals "who project evil toward other human beings by the power of thought" (Kilpatrick and Kilpatrick 1967b, 170). The arcane rite of "remaking tobacco" to counteract the machinations of such malignant forces is largely confined to full-time practitioners of Cherokee magic because it involves cultivating a special species of *Nicotiana Rustica* L., which is grown in secret and magically strengthened by its exposure to the illuminating rays of the eastern sun (a lengthy description of these procedures can be found in Kilpatrick and Kilpatrick 1967b, 8–12).

The medicine man Egi, who recorded this formula, also offered his own personal insight about the potency of this highly charged ritual: "Smoke anytime, anywhere. If Smoke touches offenders, they will quit [their] evil designs." There is a similar formula attributed to the folk healer Dlanus Toyanisi, published in Kilpatrick and Kilpatrick 1967b, 170–71.

Text 17 "To Compel an Enemy to Forget"

odahlí	*egwatsú:hi*	*aye:hlí*	*degaduyu:sga*
lake	great	middle	I wade

digwalá:sde:ni	*tsuné:gv*	*aye:hlí*	*nido:tsustidégá*
my feet	white	middle	I can see them

gohú:sdi	*sgi:yeliséhi*	*getsadelehú:hisdi*	*nige:sv́:na*
something	those who think [evil] of me	you will know it	never

salu:yi	*eguatsú:hi*	*aye:hlí*
underbrush	great	middle

degaduyu:sga
I wade

digwalásde:ni	*tsuné:gv*	*aye:hlí*	*nido:tsustidegá*
my feet	white	middle	I can see them

gohú:sdi	*sgi:yeliséhi*	*getsadelehó:hisdí*	*nige:sv́:na*
something	those who think [evil] of me	you will know it	never

nv́do	*egwatsú:hi*	*aye:hlí*	*degaduyu:sga*
heavenly body	great	middle	I wade

digwalásde:ni	*tsuné:gv*	*aye:hlí*	*nido:tsustidegá*
my feet	white	middle	I can see them

gohú:sdi	*sgi:yeliséhi*	*getsadelehó:hisdí*	*nige:sv́:na*
something	those who think [evil] of me	you will know it	never

odahlí	*egwatsú:hi*	*aye:hlí*	*degaduyu:sga*
mountain	great, place	middle	I wade

digwalásde:ni	*tsuné:gv*	*aye:hlí*	*nido:tsustidegá*
my feet	white	middle	I can see them

gohú:sdi	*sgi:yeliséhi*	*getsadelehó:hisdí*	*nige:sv́:ná*
something	those who think [evil] of me	you will know it	never

Free Translation

In the middle of a great lake I wade. I can see my white feet there in the middle. Those of you who think evil of me will never know it.

   In the middle of a great brushland I wade. I can see my white feet there in the middle. Those of you who think evil of me will never know it.

   In the middle of a great sun I wade. I can see my white feet there in the middle. Those of you who think evil of me will never know it.

   In the middle of a great mountain I wade. I can see my white feet there in the middle. Those of you who think evil of me will never know it.

Commentary

This formula was found in a notebook that belonged to the medicine man Dlanus Toyanisi. The manuscript appears to date to about 1920.

The symbols of the great lake, brushland, sun, and mountain are used here to great poetic effect. Shielded by this gamut of natural forces, reciters of this spell are free to continue their life journeys unhindered by the dark forces. To the Cherokee psyche the color of white celebrates a condition of tranquility and felicity. Therefore, the phrase, "I can see my white feet there in the middle," represents, metaphorically, that the reciter is now enshrined in an impervious state of psychological calm.

By magically obstructing the evil intentions that emanate from the souls of humans conjurers render them harmless. The conjurers' potential adversaries have neither the ability to vocalize their threats nor mentally to conspire against them, which is the meaning of the phrase, "Those of you who think evil of me will never know it."

Text 18   "To Forget the Dead"

ugalo:gá	*unoyuyonusgihlanv*
leaf	flood-borne

nvya:hno	*uwásgahlanvhi*	*juyágalohi*
rock, and	stuck on	bank of stream

na:sgi	*agá:nvhi*	*ali:sdodi*
that	boiled	to vomit,

nv²ghi	*tsu:sv:hidǘ*
four	overnights [days]

tsuniyo:hv:sv:hi	*dá:nadadisgv*	*u:wo:dhi*
the dead	treating	medicine

ghilo	*tsuniyo:hu:sv:hi*	*yidadá:hnvte:ha*
someone	which died, they	if someone is thinking about you

Free Translation

Take a flood-borne leaf that has been stuck on a rock. Boil it so that one can vomit. Do this for four days—the Dead Treating Medicine, if someone who is dead is thinking about you.

Commentary

Sir James Frazer's observation that the aboriginal attitude toward the dead is more "dominated by fear rather than by affection" ([1933] 1966, 10) appears to hold true in many respects. An enormous amount of ethnographic documentation suggests that many Native American societies viewed recently departed spirits as either polluting or dangerous elements, which, if not placated ritually, could wreak vengeance on the living (see the literature on the Cheyenne [Hobel 1960, 87]; the Menomini [Spindler 1989, 42]; the Seneca 158 [Wallace 1972, 99]; the Navajo, Apache, Shoshoni-Paiute, Yuman, and Piman [Hultkrantz 1981, 94]; the Paviotso [Parker 1938, 40]; Lakota [DeMallie, Jahner, and Walker 1980, 71]; Texas-Alabama and Chickasaw [Swanton 1928, 511–12]; the Ojibwe [Rohrl, personal communication); the Iroquois [Morgan [1851] 1972, 175]; the Huron [Thwaites 1847, 379] and the Choctaw [Tse:gi Ganv:hnawó:i field notes n.d.]).

Numerous theories have been put forth to explain this widespread phobia of the dead. One thesis focuses on the idea that spirits "undergo after death a great change, which affects their character and temper on the whole for the worse, rendering them touchy, irritable, prone to take offence on the slightest pretext and to visit their displeasure on the survivors" (Frazer [1933] 1966, 11).

Another explanation centers around the fear that a marooned soul "not yet reconciled to its fate" will attempt to reclaim its persona by possessing the body of the living (Sigerist 1951, 1: 137). Among the Iroquoian groups it was customary to hold feasts of the dead and the Ohgiwe ceremony as well. Although these rites functioned as solemn commemorative occasions, they also served as social mechanisms to ward off lingering spirits who, "frustrated in their longings for food and companionship, were apt to bother people in their dreams and even to plague survivors with sickness and misfortune" (Wallace 1972, 99). Iroquois herbalists used to prescribe a tea made from *gaiyonwagras* ('stink guts'), which was believed to be effective against "bothering" from the spirit world (Shimony 1989, 149, 163 n. 4).

The Creek Indians employed both smoked cedar leaves and ginseng to drive out pestering spirits. "The sovereign deterrent for ghosts," according to one source, however, was *Hitci pakpagi*, or tobacoo bloom (Swanton 1928, 662).

Although Cherokees semantically distinguish in their language between the ghost of an animal (*udhá:li*) and that of a human (*asgí:na*), they acknowledge that both spiritual entities can cause problems for the living. Cherokees, like their Muskogean counterparts, use smoked cedar leaves to ward off malicious haunting spirits. As a safeguard, mourners at funerals would often drop cedar leaves (about three inches long) on the casket. There was a folk belief that anyone who attended a funeral without smoking him or herself thoroughly with cedar would become ill within seven days (Tse:gi Ganv:hnawó:i field notes n.d.).

Cherokees, historically, have placed great import on the medium of dreams (cf. Mooney and Olbrechts 1932, 35–37). Generally, ghosts who invade a person's somnambulistic state are regarded as harbingers of doom. The present text, preserved in the Uwe:da:sadhi Sa:wali papers, appears to be a preventive measure against such nocturnal visitations.

Besides this "Going to the Water" ritual, other folk methodologies are thought to be effective against "bad" dreams. One is to build a small fire and smoke one's face. If this measure proves ineffective, then the patient is advised to "go out just as you wake up, look up at the Pleiades and tell them to take a certain direction" (Tse:gi Ganv:hnawó:i field notes n.d.).

The eastern Cherokees purged themselves of poltergeists by conducting rituals similar to those described in the above text. One such procedure is outlined in the unpublished field notes of Frans Olbrechts: the troubled patient is to boil seven young sprouts of *no:tsi* ('table mountain pine' [*Pinus pungens* Lamb.]). Then, early in the morning, the individual is to drink this decoction and expurgate its contents into a flowing stream (Kilpatrick and Kilpatrick, "Eastern Cherokee Ethnobotany," n.d.).

There is some ethnographic evidence that young Cherokees, apprenticing themselves to medicine men, would ingest a decoction composed of dank stream leaves to improve their memory and overall vitality (Mooney and Olbrechts 1932, 101). Ironically, the strategy of the above spell is to deploy the mixture not as a stimulant but as a depressant.

This nineteenth-century spell must have been thought by its peers to have a far-ranging utility, for a note appended to this weathered text, written by a modern-day medicine man, indicates that the patient is to use a "bunch of leaves as big as a fist." It should be pointed out that, as efficacious as these various remedies are in nullifying troublesome spirits, two generations of magical practitioners in Oklahoma hold firm to the belief that a spell cast by a dead conjuror is practically incurable (Tse:gi Ganv:hnawó:i field notes n.d.).

Text 19   "To Hide"

Caption

adádelisdo:i	i:gawé:sdi
secretive	to say it, one

Spell

qwatloya	gal'ú:la²di	díneqwa	gv:hnáge
[?]	above	mole	black

hagatso:dhani:ga
you have just come to blow on it

sa:gwo	ga:da	gínatsánvsgi
one	earth	you and I dressed up

ga:da	ga:da nvwatlvdhani:ga
earth	I have just come to cover up [with earth]

ha	u:sinu:liyu
ha	quickly, very

Free Translation

A spell to hide one.

Qwatloya, Black Mole above
Very Quickly you have just
come to blow on it.
You and I are dressed
as one, the earth. Ha!
I have just came to cover up
very quickly with the earth!

Commentary

This incantation transcribed from the Uwe:da:sadhi Sa:wali papers belongs to that genre of hiding spells known as *di:da:n(v)dí:yisdo² dhí:yi*

('to miss them with, one'). To actualize its full potency this incantation should be recited four times (a variant of this text, attributed to a female folk healer named Lu:si Wahhya, appeared in Kilpatrick and Kilpatrick 1967b, 166).

My informants could not offer any plausible explanation for the word, *qwatloya*. The placement of this enigmatic word in the very beginning of the prayer (a section usually reserved for addresses to supernatural entities, particularly those who inhabit the uppermost mythological realms), however, leads me to speculate that it is some sort of celestial deity.

Text 20   "For Protection While Traveling"

[To be sung]

a:sgaya	gigagé:i	igv:yi	walehv:gv
men	red	first	he's putting it in front

ada:nvdho?	góghi(i)sdi
soul	to smoke it, one

[To be said]

dhlv:datsi	gigagé:i	igv:yi	walehv:ga
panther	red, it	first	he's putting it in front

tsi:sdets(i)	dalo:ni	igv:yi	walehv:ga
mouse	yellow, it	first	he's putting it in front

o:gana	gv:hnagé:i	igv:yi	walehv:ga
groundhog	black, it	first	he's putting it in front

gi:hli	gv:hnagé:i	igv:yi	walehv:ga
dog	black, it	first	he's putting it in front

Free Translation

The Red Men are putting the soul in front to cover it in smoke.
First, The Red Panther is putting it in front!
First, the Yellow Mouse is putting it in front!

First, the Black Groundhog is putting it in front!
First, the Black Dog is putting it in front!

Commentary

Historically, foot travel into Indian territory was a hazardous undertaking. One might be bushwacked by lurking bandits or mauled by some wild animal. Worst yet, one might encounter some dreadful apparition from the spirit world.

This potent protective charm, designed to be both sung and recited, was dictated to my late father in 1963 by Uwo:digé Gigagé:i, who was widely regarded by his contemporaries as one of the preeminent Cherokee folk healers of his time. The verb in the original text, *walehvgv,* is, I suspect, a ritualistic corruption of *wahvs:gv* ('to put it first, to lead').

Text 21   "For Protection While Traveling"

Caption

nv:no:hi	vdovi	ahl(i)sdé:hl(v)do²dí
road	going	to help one

Spell

ha:niyu	ha:niyu
get out of the way!	get out of the way!

sge²	odahlí	tsugv:yiyi
listen	mountain	at first

iyv:dvgwo	ni:dodó:gwadunvhi
far, just	over there, I arose from

ha	nv:no:hi	tsune:gv	dagina:wadi
ha	pathways	white, you	are lying, they

ha	daksi:gwo	ige:sé:i
ha	terrapin, just	it was

nv:do   *dunanu:gotsv:hi*
sun   earliest rising

ha   *nv:no:hi:gwo*   *aye:hliyu*
ha   pathways, just   middle, very

*uda:n(v)do*ˀ   *de:duligv:haseyásvli:ga*
soul, his   they have just come to chop up

ha   *nv:ya*   *igáhvsgi*
ha   rock   sayer

nv:do   *dunanu:gotsv:hi*   *ha*   *nv:no:hi*   *aye:hliyu*
sun   earliest rising   ha   pathways   middle, very

*duda:n(v)do*ˀ   *doduligv:haseyásvli:ga*
soul, his   he has just come to chop up

4
[four times]

Free Translation

To help one going on a road.

Get out of the way! Get out of the way!
Listen! From the farthest mountain over there I arose.
Ha! White Pathways you are lying upon.
Ha! it was the Terrapin at the earliest sun rising.
The pathways in the very middle of his soul they have come to chop
    up!
Ha! It was the Rock-Sayer at the earliest sun rising.
Ha! The pathways in the very middle of his soul he has just come to
    chop up!
[The spell is to be recited four times.]

Commentary

The deities addressed here, the Terrapin and the Rock-Sayer, are rarely
invoked in Cherokee magical spells. The protective armor of the Ter-

rapin along with its ability to snap off offending insults may be the key to its appearance here. The role of the Rock-Sayer remains something of an enigma.

In comparison to other formulae this text bristles with threatening and aggressive images. By "chopping up the very middle of his soul" reciters seek to destablize the psyche of any enemy who might confront them on a journey.

One is to recite the text four times. There is no accompanying ritual. The medicine man who dictated this protective spell qualified it as a "real good one."

Traveling spells often exhibit complicated wording and unusual allusions. An older example, discovered in the papers of Uwe:da:sadhi Sa:wali, demonstrates this tendency. Captioned "To say while walking upon the Road," the separtite text goes:

Text 21a

Earthworm!
You and I are clad as one with soil.
Very quickly, I have just come to join You underground.
Upon the Road I will be rolled up like a ball.

Leech!
Very quickly, the Road now!
I have just come upon the Road in order to have faith!

Text 22   "Night Walkers"

Caption

tso:la	sv:no:yi	ane:dó:hi	ugv:wahli
tobacco	night	walkers	for the purpose of

go:dhlvhiso?dhi
to remake, it

Spell

Gha sge!
now listen

na:gwo	ha?dhv:gá:ni:gá		higayv:li
now	you have just come to hear		ancient, one

tso:la	gvyásvgalv́dani:ga
tobacco	I have just come to put in one's hand

gahl(i)gwo	iyanila:sdala:gi
seven	each of the clans

u:ya	i:gawé:sdi	nv:no:hi
evil	to say it, one	road

Free Translation

To remake tobacco for the purpose of night walkers

Now! Listen, You have just come
to hear, Ancient One
I have just come to put tobacco in my hand.
Seven Clans!
Evil, one says while on the road.

Commentary

The most dreaded apparition to accost a traveler on a lonely stretch of
road would be a *sv:no:yi ane:dó:hí* ('night walker'). Ceremonially remade
tobacco is the only certain safeguard against these vampiric creatures.
This formula was recorded in the papers of Uwe:da:sadhi Sa:wali and
dates to late nineteenth century.

Text 23   "To Cause Someone to Move"

Caption

tso:la	go:dhlvhiso?dhi	gó:ghisdi
tobacco	to remake	to smoke it, one

su:nalé:i	go:dhlvhiso?dhi
early morning	remake

Spell

gho:ga	gv:hnagé:i	detsusdí:skoni:ga
crow	black, it	you have just come to mourn?

ha	u:sanu:liyu	gedó[luˀ] seˀsdani:gá
ha	quickly, very	I have just come to visit

Ka! Ka! Ka! Kaaa!

ha	dine	uhi:soˀdí	tsa[eˀ][lvˀ]wadise:sdi
ha	you	loneliness	to stand by, yourself

Free Translation

Smoke "remade" tobacco. Remake early in the morning.

Black Crow! You have just come to mourn!
Ha! Very Quickly I have just come to visit!
Ka! Ka! Ka! Kaaa!
Don't stand by yourself in Loneliness!

Commentary

This text is designed to remove a pesky neighbor from your vacinity. Its author, Uwodigé Gigagé:i, dictated the spell to my late father in July 1963.

The instructions are that the reciter is ceremonially to "remake" tobacco. But one is cautioned not to hold the renewed tobacco up to the sunlight. Then the reciter of the text goes halfway toward the victim's house and delivers the spell prolonging the final "Kaaa!" in the third line. After this has been accomplished, the reciter blows smoke toward the abode of his offensive neighbor. The ritual is repeated for four days, and can be performed at anytime (day or night) during that interval.

There were considerable orthographic problems in deciphering this text. My informants believe that the original word, *sejustskoniga*, is a ritualistic corruption of 'you have just came to mourn.' The last phrase, "don't stand by yourself in loneliness," means that the neighbor should "get the feeling" (*tsa:dawadi:sesdi*) that his presence is unwanted and quickly move to a more receptive location.

Text 24 "To Fix Tobacco for Use at Night to Repel Evil Ones"

sdelv:gi   *ani:do:sgi*
to help one [?]   passing by, they [?]

Free Translation

To help when they pass by [?]

Commentary

Despite its very lengthy title one is immediately struck by the brevity of this spell. Cherokee practitioners maintain that the efficacy of their magic does not depend upon the length of a particular text but upon their skill, imagination, and experience. My father recorded this "To Turn One Aside" spell from Uwodigé Gigagé:i on June 12, 1963.

It is noteworthy that Uwodigé, who was one of the most respected medicomagical practitioners in northeastern Oklahoma, did not know the exact meaning of the words. One of my informants has suggested that *sdelv:gi* is an abortive form of the verb, 'to help' and insists that *ani:dó:sgi* is a corruption of 'passing by, they.' There is a faint possibility that the word is a ritualism of *ani:sados:sgi* ('forces').

Unlike the preceeding text, this rite is to be used only at night. According to the instructions, one prepares "remade" tobacco and then recites this spell before he or she lights the pipe. One either blows the resulting smoke at the house or encircles the residence with the fumes. If someone evil is occupying the house, the smoke quickly drives out the intruder.

5

"To Lower One's Soul"

As a result of the aura of criminality that surrounds them, it has been observed that "certain classes of Cherokee formulae are exceedingly difficult to acquire, since they constitute the closely guarded arcane of the medicine man's art" (Jack F. Kilpatrick, the Dlanus Toyanisi manuscript, n.d.). Mooney and Olbrechts comment further: "rarely a medicine man will own that he knows one, or even that he has one in his possession" (1932, 154).

The present set of "To Lower One's Soul" texts fall into this category because they represent instruments whose express purpose is to destroy human life. To safeguard their heinous content from unauthorized exposure these "bad" formulae are generally mislabeled or simply left untitled. Because of their grave and irreversible consequences, life-threatening spells, such as those presented here, were traditionally the last incantations to be taught to an apprentice *dida:hnvwi:sgi* (Mooney and Olbrechts 1932, 100).

Text 25 "To Destroy an Enemy"

e:hihyvga	*tsada:n(v)do*	
bring me	your soul	

tsi:sgili	*gv:hnagé:i*	*sv:no:yi*
owl	black	night

sv:no:yi	*ditsadó:idá*	
night	your name	

tsana:hwi	*u:hyohá*	
your heart	it hunts	

e:hihyvga   *tsada:n(v)do*
bring me   your soul

tsi:sgili   *uwo:digé*   *sv:no:yi*
owl   brown, it   night

sv:no:yi   *ditsadó:idá*
night   your name

tsana:hwi   *u:hyohá*
your heart   it hunts

e:hihyvga   *tsada:n(v)do*
bring me   your soul

tsi:sgili   *dalo:nige*   *sv:no:yi*
owl   yellow, it   night

sv:no:yi   *ditsadó:idá*
night   your name

tsana:hwi   *u:hyohá*
your heart   it hunts

e:hihyvga   *tsada:n(v)do*
bring me   your soul

tsi:sgili   *une:ga*   *sv:no:yi*
owl   white, it   night

sv:no:yi   *ditsadó:idá*   *tsana:hwi*   *u:hyohá*
night   your name   your heart   it hunts

Free Translation

Bring me your soul. I am a black owl of the night.
Your name is Night. It [the owl] hunts your heart.
Bring me your soul. I am a brown owl of the night.
Your name is Night. It [the owl] hunts your heart.
Bring me your soul. I am a yellow owl of the night.

Your name is Night. It [the owl] hunts your heart.
Bring me your soul. I am a white owl of the night.
Your name is Night. It [the owl] hunts your heart.

Commentary

Because this is the consummate witch spell, no physical directives are necessary to implement it. Thought, alone, is enough. As Mooney and Olbrechts note, a fully realized conjuror "who has attained the summit of occult power" can destroy a victim simply "by reciting an incantation against him" (1932, 87). The color scheme in the four statements, a progression from black to white, may possibly symbolize the gradual success of the spell. This is a common psychological device employed by Cherokee practitioners of magic.

Cherokees regard all species of owl as supernatural messengers. The favorite avian form of metaphorized witches and sorcerers, however, is believed to be the long-eared owl (*Asio wilsonianus* (Kilpatrick and Kilpatrick 1970, 95). Undoubtedly, this embodiment of evil is celebrated here in this 1920 text recorded by the medicine man Dlanus Toyanisi:

Text 26

Caption

dudóhv	*igv:yi*
name,[his or her]	first

Spell

Gha!	*sv:no:yi*	*wahuhi*	*tsa:lilesvha*
listen	night	owl	take it away with you

Gha!	*sv:no:yi*	*tsajuli*	*tsa:lilesvha*
listen	night	sapsucker	take it away with you

Gha!	*sv:no:yi*	*huhu*	*tsa:lilesvha*
listen	night	yellow mockingbird	take it away with you

Gha!	*sv:no:yi*	*tsada:nvdo*	*tsa:lilesvha*
listen	night	your soul	take it away with you

Free Translation

[One says first the name of the victim.]

Listen! Night Owl, take it away with you!
Listen! Night Sapsucker, take it away with you!
Listen! Night Mockingbird, take it away with you!
Listen! Night, Your [the victim's] soul, take it away with you!

Commentary

The stealing away of one's soul by necrotic forces is a familiar theme in "bad" formulae. This brief, but intense curse was penned by the medicine man Jackson Standingdeer, who once served as the minister of the Sycamore Baptist Church. The text bears the date 1946.

The following two examples are not of the spells themselves but are the most rare occurence in the written specimens of western Cherokee medicomagical literature: the actual instructions for implementing these life-threatening spells.

The first set of instructions is brief and is taken from a medicine book belonging to Dlanus Toyanisi:

Text 27 "To Kill"

tsu:sga	*dhlugv́:i*
postoak	tree

ahla:lesdi
to make holes

de:talesv	*ghvdhó:dhi*
holes	to use, one

hna:na:no	*ga:nudi*	*ahnuwo:gi*	*ni:ganvhisv*
where, and	to put, one	cloth	full-length

yv:wi	*asdá:ya:hno*	*asdudi*
person	hard, and	to close it, one

Free Translation

One makes holes near a post oak tree where one puts in a full-length cloth, and this person closes it [the hole] up completely.

Commentary

The ritual burial of ceremonial objects often includes medicine books, which are occasionally squirreled away in holes in trees or placed in glass jars underneath the ground. The complete ritual significance of this act is made clear from the final set of instructions, which comes from the papers of the nineteenth-century Cherokee medicine man Uwe:da:sadhi Sa:wali:

Text 28   "To Kill"

u:nvdodi	*dida:hnese:sgi*	*hi²a²*
to do, they	conjurors, they	this

watsi:la	*agi:svdi*
saliva	to be taken, one

ulitsi:stludonvhi	*ga:nasda*	*ghvdhó:dhi*
where he spits	stick	to use it, one

kanv:sogwo	*svlidv*	*sa:gwo*	*u:nidi*
wild parsnip	cane	one	to put down

igv:yi	*a²hni*	*ditlvno*	*asda:ya*	*a:sdvdi*
first	this	side	tight	shut

tsisgo:ya	*gado:hi*	*ane:hi*
worms	earth-place	residers, they

na:hna	*di:yodi*	*jusdayohida*	*jutlv:danuda*
there	to hunt them one,	lightning-strips	struck

hinu:sgi   *na:hna*   *svlida*   *digaladi:sdi*
a few   there   cane   to put them in

ale dinulvdi:sgi   *ale gha:natsisde:tsi*
and dirt-daubers   and wasp

hna:gwo   *na:sgi*   *niga:dv*   *yasgwadv:*
now   that   all   when finished:

hna:gwo   *i:nage*   *hwigalohi:sdi*
now   woods   to go there, one

jusdayohida   *dhlugv́*   *u:lidatlv*   *asgo:sdi*
lightning-struck   tree   beyond   to dig, one

ga:do:hi   *nv:ya*   *wo:digé*   *ga:do:qwala*   *i:yú:sdi*   *nvdv:di*   *hawí:ni*
earth-place   stone   brown   earth, clay   like   to put   deep
                                                                                     there

hna:gwo:na   *yasdu:nonv*   *asdá:ya*   *walasidi*   *agadigeni*
now, and   closing   tight   to put one's   heel
                                               foot down

gú:ʔdi   *hna:gwo:no*   *nv:ya*   *gv:hnagé*   *wa:di*
to use   now, and   stone   black   to lay there, one

hna:gwo:no   *gódhlvdí*   *vyosdi:sgv*   *sv:dolv*   *iga:dui*
now, and   to make a fire   to erase   walked, one   on top

hna:gwo:no   *ga:hl(i)gwo:gi*   *iyv:sv*   *u:yotlehi:sdi*
now, and   seven   days   to die, he/she

hna:gwo:no   *na:sgi*   *nu:lista:nvna*   *yi:gi*
now, and   that   not happen   if

hna:gwo   *owa:sv*   *ahl(i)sdéhl(v)doʔdí*
now   oneself   to help, one

i:nage   *u:sdi*   *uweyú*   *hwigalo:hisdi*
woods   designated   stream   to go there, one

ahnuwo:gi	*une:gv*	*sa:gwo*	*ale*	*dha?li*	*iyutli:lodv*	*i:ganv:hí:dv*
cloth	white	one	and	two	yards	in length

ga:hligwo:gi	*uniné:ga*	*ade:la*	*sa:gwo*
seven	white ones	beads	one

ale	*dha?li*	*iyutli:lodv*	*ahnuwo:gi*
and	two	yards	cloth

gigagé	*ale*	*gv:hnagégwo*	*yi:gi*	*ale*
red	or	black, very	if it is	and

ga:hl(i)gwo:gi	*ani:gagé*	*ade:la*	*ale*
seven	red ones	beads	and

anv:hnagé:gwo
black ones, very

yi:gi	*ha:sgino*	*ani:gagé*	*ade:la*
if it is	that	red ones	beads

a?gadi:sa	*di:tlv*
right	toward

Free Translation

The conjurors do this. Take the saliva where one spits. Use a wild parsnip to put it into the earth where the worms live. Hunt out a few
lightning-struck strips [of wood] from the ground. Put them in [a bas-
ket?] with dirt-daubers and wasps. Now, when all that is finished, go to
the remote woods to a lightning-struck tree. Beyond it, dig a hole with a
brown claylike stone. Put them [the strips, dirt-daubers, and wasps]
deep, now, and close it tight, putting one's heel down [to secure the
hole] and put a black stone [to mark the spot]. Then make a fire on top
of the hole to erase where one walked.

   In seven days he or she will die. If this does not happen, to help
oneself go to the woods near a small stream. [Bring] a white cloth,
which is one or two yards in length, and seven white beads, or a red or
black cloth, which is one or two yards in length, with seven red or black
beads toward the spot. (The conjuror is then expected to recite a vari-

ant of one of these "Lower The Soul" incantations near the stream. This auxiliary procedure will bolster the former spell and make it lethal).

Commentary

This deadly ritual, whose purpose is *tsuní:hisdoˀdí* ('which to kill with, they'), is also recorded in Mooney 1891, 391–93. The above text appears to follow the eastern Cherokee procedures rather closely.

The role that wild parsnip, *Pastinaca sativa* L., plays in this nefarious rite is puzzling. A variant of this native biennial plant, *Pratensis* pers., however, is reputed to be poisonous (cf. Olbrechts 1930, 550).

An equally venomous spell is transcribed in English from the papers of Uwe:da:sadhi Sa:wali. Here, the main ingredient is remade *tso: lagayú:li* ('ancient tobacco'):

Text 28a

Red Thunder, quickly, You have just come to claw out the souls of men! Red Panther, quickly, You and I have just bent down to enter into the souls of men!
They will be inclining them toward the Nightland!
[They are named.]

To activate the magic reciters mix *tso:lagayú:li* with a store-bought brand of tobacco. For four days they remake this substance early in the morning while fasting all day. On the fourth day preparers begin to smoke this powerful strain, pausing to recite the above text and, no doubt, blowing its poisonous fumes in the direction of the victim. Uwe:da:sadhi's remarks are arresting: "Truly, indeed, it will create evil for a person. Anything that one decides is to happen, will happen."

Text 29   "To Trap Night Walkers"

sv:no:yi	*ane:dó:hi*	*disadvdii*	*gvge:dino*	
night	walkers	to trap	to use	

ge:sv	*selu iyú:sdi*	*kane:sga*	*dighvdhó:dhí*	*judawohili*
it is	corn like	straw	to use	to overtake

idi:ganv:hídv	*sa:gwo*	*nv:no:hi*	*ge:sv*
long	one	road	it is

ga:hligwo:gi	*i:diga:i*	*tso?i*	*idiga: nv:wo:dhi*
seven	that much	three	to say it, medicine

si:ga	*nv:ya*	*tsu:sv́:hidv*	*dige:dvsdi*
all day	stone	overnight	stand there up [as in fence post].

Free Translation

One uses it to trap Night Walkers.
It is a cornlike stalk one uses to overtake them
One uses seven of them on a long road.
One stands a stone up like a fence post.
One says the medicine three times, that much.

Commentary

These cryptic instructions, which inform about how to dispatch *sv:no:yi ane:dó:hi* ('night walkers about, they'), were found in the papers of Uwe:da:sadhi Sa:wali. To "lower the soul" of a witch one must resort to counteractive magic. Generally, witches are vulnerable to magically empowered arrows, sharpened stakes, or bullets that can pierce their flesh. According to the authors of the *"Swimmer Manuscript,"* to shoot a witch one must mix the ingredients of a certain plant [not described in the monograph, but probably spider root] with the gun powder. In addition, a human hair, extracted from the crown of the assassin's head, must be entwined around the bullet to render it efficacious (Mooney and Olbrechts 1932, 31).

Because witches are notorious for shape shifting, the hunter must be able to perceive the *tsi:sgili* in its human form. This is accomplished "by fasting until sunset for seven days, drinking an infusion of the same root to which the witches owe their power" (Mooney and Olbrechts 1932, 31).

The root referred to, here, by Mooney and Olbrechts is *ahó:liyé:hv:sgí* ('it has it in its mouth'). This plant, whose botanical name is *Sagittaria latifolia* Willd., is not used by the Cherokee for medicinal purposes but is employed instead only to heighten supernatural abilities. According to my late parent's field notes, "The name would appear to be an elision of *ahó:li* ('mouth') and *é:hv:sgí* ('it that resides') and derives from the resemblance of the flower of the plant to a beetle-like insect with an object in its mouth" (Kilpatrick and Kilpatrick, "Eastern Cherokee Ethnobotany," n.d.).

Text 30   "To Destroy Wicked Ones"

Caption

unetsu:tsidv	*hi²a² go:wé:la*
wicked ones	this written

tsu:sdayohida	*tsulv:dalvda*	*ge:dvsdi*	*gohú:sdi*	*asadvdo:di*
lightning-struck	strips	to stick	something	to trip, one upright

udayu:lohisdi:i	*de:ganvnv*	*di:ganvdi*	*nv:no:hi*
to pass, one	roads	to put down	road

Spell

Gha!	*nv:no:hi*	*tsune:gv*	*ayv*	*digwatsanv:gi*
listen!	road white,	you	I am	dressed

huhu	*gv:hnagé:i*	*duna:hwi*	*detaso:hwisiga*
yellow mockingbird	black	his heart	you have just brought it down

huhu	*gv:hnagé:i*	*duna:hwi*	*deta:ginutisga*
yellow mockingbird	black	his heart	you have just leaped upon it

a²sdi	*gigagé:i*	*duna:hwi*	*hlanu:sdaneli:gá*
thread	red	his heart	you have just come to wrap around it

ga:hligwo:gi	*usvhi*
seven	all night

hiyidlaquv	*halv:gidiga*	*e:hlawe²*
(personal name)	you have just come to untie it	quietly

nudv:tanvda   *dudanvdheli:do:lǘ:hi*
not to go away   thinker of me

aᵓsdi   *tsune:gv*
thread   white

nidogv:wada:nawade:gesdi
he will be strung up like a web

na:gwo   *dine*   *ase*   *dudelitsonvhi*
now   you   must   be out of sight

gv:hnagé:i   *gvwadv:sadise:sdi*
black   to serve it, it will be

uyo:iyu   *aᵓdi:ha*
evil, very   says, it

Free Translation

This is written for the Wicked Ones. One is to stick something like lightning-struck strips [of wood] to trip one as they pass by the roads. Put it down on the road.

Now! I am dressed in the White Pathway!
Black Yellow Mockingbird,
You have just brought down his heart!
Black Yellow Mockingbird,
You have just leaped upon his heart!
Red Thread,
You have just come to wrap around his heart!
Seven Times! All Night!
Hiyidlaquv? (Personal Name?)
You have just come to quietly untie the Thinker before he goes away!
He will be strung up like a web with White Thread!
Now! He must be out of sight.
The Very Black Evil will serve him, it says!

Commentary

This potent formula, designed to destroy witches, bears a strong resem-blance to a text recorded in Kilpatrick and Kilpatrick 1967b, 145, which is labeled "To Counteract an Incantation: To Make One Forget." Morever, both texts were transcribed from the papers of the same individual—Uwe:da:sadhi Sa:wali.

One recites this spell while placing seven deadly splinters of lightning-struck wood along a trail a suspected *tsi:sgili* is known to frequent. For the "wicked ones" death is instantaneous.

An equivalent set of "To Lower the Soul" formulae exists among the eastern Cherokee. One such specimen was collected in 1948 by researcher Frank G. Speck from Allen Long, who was a relative of Will West Long, the Cherokee informant who contributed so much ethnographic information about the eastern Cherokee folk beliefs to Speck and John Witthoff during the 1940s and early 1950s.

This life-threatening incantation, (which was characteristically mislabeled as "This One Is Very Difficult") was translated by my late mother, Anna G. Kilpatrick, in February 1974. The accompanying note explains: "'This one makes one sick', so said those who lived long ago. This is to be said at night fall."

Text 30a

Now! Quickly, Quietly it has risen!
I walked and stepped on it!
Name was Ginsi (the person for whom
this magic is to be used).

Now, the big red rattler is blazing!
It is not dressed in Blue!
I have stepped on someone's heart!
It is well. This is the kind I step on.——
(the name to be inserted by the person using it).

This is the straight path that is blocked.
Now, it's undressed the red clothes, it is blazing!
Now, it has come to turn the path, now the path fades!
Now, the path will be there through the very deep night!

The path will be lost forever, never to return!
Somewhere in the woods, the legs will be trembling!
The smell will be Black,
Over there, in its resting place, it has gone down again.

The Mole is awakening him (or her),
it is clothing it with Evil.
He (the Mole) is saying: "It will be this way now
To rise again, he must step on someone's whole heart!"

    This unusual incantation bristles with the vibrant energy of the conjuror's art. The imagery sets up a telling contrast between the blazing, venomous rattlesnake power of the reciter and the dwindling vitality of the victim, whose path (a metaphor here for life force) is "to be lost forever, never to return."

    The pungency of decay is woven into the funereal stanza. The corpse will be awakened only by the blind, burrowing mole, who will tactfully remind the victim that the only way to regain his life energies is to perpetrate witchcraft ("to step on" [to capture] an innocent person's heart [soul]).

    This formula is singular in the perversity of its motives, for the victim is not just condemned to the state of death but to the state of the undead (e.g., in Cherokee folk belief witches are not considered to be "human") (cf. Fogelson 1979, 87). To my knowledge no other formula in the entire medicomagical literature of the Cherokee approaches this sadistic dimension.

6

"To Elevate One's Soul"

Cherokee Purification Texts

The primary symbols of everlasting purity among the Cherokee are the natural elements of fire and water. Fire, personified as "the ancient white one," holds a special place of reverence in Cherokee religious thought.

Historically, ceremonial fires were never extinquished by water but were symbolically "renewed" by rekindling the flames during such celebrations as the Green Corn dances (Hudson 1976, 318). After their removal to Indian Territory in the 1830s, the ancient ceremonial fire was brought from the east by the survivors of the Trail of Tears because it symbolized a continuation of the "old ways."

Trees set ablaze by lightning (celestial fire) were thought to have special protective powers. As a result, lightning-struck wood was considered to be the most potent magical element to eradicate witches.

Linguists have long observed that cultures which have an important relationship with some object or event will possess many words in their language to celebrate that special connection (e.g., eskimos vis-à-vis *snow*) (Chaika 1994, 350). To the Cherokee mind bathing one's body or spirit in wet, flowing water is the ultimate expression of human purity. As a consequence, it has been estimated that more than one hundred thousand verb forms in Cherokee describe the concept "to wash" (cf. Scancarelli 1994). This singular attitude can be contrasted with that of the Tlingit Indians, whose concepts of purification embody the qualities of hardness, heaviness, and dryness (Kan 1989, 54–56).

"Going to the Water" (*amó:hi* ['water place'] *atsú:sdi* ['to go and return, one']), an aboriginal rite involving a symbolic baptism in a flowing stream, is the most prevalent purification ceremony among the Cherokees. Judging from the sheer numbers of such texts, no Cherokee medicine book would be considered complete without, at least, one such formula. Given the importance the Cherokee invested in this riparian ceremony, it is curious that no lengthy monograph on the subject has ever appeared in print. Despite this fact there is some ethnographic reportage of the rites themselves, with Mooney's early description being the most preeminent:

> Going to the Water . . . is one of their most frequent medico-religious ceremonies, and is performed at a great variety of occasions, such as at each new moon, before eating the new food at the green corn dance, before the medicine dance and other ceremonial dances and after the ball play, in connection with the prayers for a long life, to counteract the effects of bad dreams or the evil spells of an enemy, and as a part of the regular treatment in various diseases. The details of the ceremony are very elaborate and vary accordingly to the purpose for which it is performed, but in all cases both shaman and client are fasting from the previous evening, the ceremony being generally performed just at daybreak. The bather usually dips completely under the water four or seven times, but in some cases it is sufficient to pour water from the hand upon the head and breast (Mooney 1891, 335).

The purpose of the "Going to the Water" texts transcribed here are threefold: to determine an individual's longevity (text 31); to protect a client from the ill effects of being conjured (text 32); and to promote the physical health of a patient (text 33). The metaphysical rationale behind this Cherokee obsession with purification bears examination.

Cherokee Notions of Purity

According to the tenets of aboriginal Cherokee thought, order in the cosmos is sustained, primarily, by two human behaviors: balance and purification. Harmony with the universe is maintained by individuals practicing certain modes of ethical action. Especially important to the Cherokee ethos is that an individual exhibit behaviors of reciprocity, which manifest, in social terms, as mutual concern and mutual respect for their kinsmen and their fellow creatures on earth.

The Cherokees had a highly circumscribed set of moral precepts that outlined social taboos and transgressions. Many of the Cherokee notions about symbolic purity and spiritual defilement emanated from their basic attitudes about the control of bodily functions. This is not surprising because anthropologists have long recognized that the human body "provides a basic model for all symbolism. There is hardly any pollution which does not have some primary physiological reference" (Douglas 1966, 193).

Historically, Cherokees demarcated their various moral categories of "clean" and "unclean" by regulating diet, by separating the sexes during critical periods, by avoiding physical contact with the dead, and by controlling the use of psychic power. It was believed that careful observance of each of these symbolic categories would not only contribute to an individual's health but would also aid in the larger maintenance of the whole metaphysical system.

According to various ethnographic sources, a compulsory taboo centered around the digestion of certain foods. For instance, it was thought to be particularly repugnant and dangerous to one's health to eat carnivorous animals such as hogs, wolves, panthers, foxes, wild dogs, or polecats (Adair [1775], 1930, 139). In addition, there were powerful strictures against eating predatory birds such as buzzards, crows, cranes, fishing hawks, owls, and eagles (Adair [1775], 1930, 137; Gilbert 1943, 346). The flesh of mammals or reptiles that burrowed underground, such as moles and snakes, was also strictly forbidden (Adair [1775], 1930, 139). Finally, there were piscatory restrictions against eating eels, catfish, and garfish (Gilbert 1943, 346).

As in Old Testament societies, females in a Cherokee community were sequestered during certain potent periods surrounding their cycles of procreation. Seven days after childbirth and during their periods of menstruation Cherokee women were considered "unclean" and were kept apart from their male counterparts (Adair [1775], 1930, 127; Gilbert 1943, 293).

A violation of this code was thought to have serious health consequences. Among the eastern Cherokee it was thought that a pregnant or menstruating woman could make a male ill either by staring at him, by standing close to him, or by preparing food for him when in this impure condition. Males weakened by this situation were advised to chew the root of gané:lidá ('pregnant, she') (golden alexander [Zizea aurea L.]) and then rub the juice from this root over the various parts of their bodies, especially "where his soul is" (in the general area of the heart). Should the patient be too weakened to conduct this ritual himself, then another individual, not necessarily a folk healer, could perform the appropriate actions (Kilpatrick and Kilpatrick, "Eastern Cherokee Ethnobotany," n.d.).

During periods of ritual warfare Cherokee soldiers were also considered to be a dangerous and polluting social element. Before their engagement, the warriors were segregated from the community and underwent rites designed to enflame their murderous passions. After their return from the battlefield, these same Cherokee warriors underwent three or four days of isolation to purify them from their "unclean" emotional state (cf. Hudson 1976, 320–21).

Besides these two polluting agents, the aboriginal Cherokee scrupulously avoided coming in physical contact with corpses: "The Cheerake [sic] . . . observe this law of purity in so strict a manner, as not to touch the corpse of their nearest relation. . . . The fear of pollution . . . keeps them also from burying their dead" (Adair [1775], 1930, 133). To restrict the spread of the contamination each Cherokee community selected one individual to dispose of a corpse. After the burial, this same individual destroyed the personal belongings of the deceased and made a new fire of "cedar boughs and goldenrod weed" to purify the house (Gilbert 1943, 347). The official's final act was to conduct the grieving family to a flowing stream where they were given an emetic and then were ritually submerged seven times in the water while facing east and west (Gilbert 1943, 348). To symbolize the achievement of a purified state the family then donned new clothes. They, however, were still kept in isolation for four days as an added precaution (Gilbert 1943, 348).

The Cherokee abhorrence of the dead was equally shared by the Creeks (Hudson 1976, 343), the Paviotso (Parker 1938, 39), the Maliseet-Passamaquoddy (Erickson 1978, 130), as well as by the Tlingit (Kan 1989, 106) as well. Exposure to the dead was thought to be responsible for a variety of physical ailments. The Creek Indian attributed fevers and aches in the leg joints to the activities of spirits of the dead (Swanton 1928, 651–52); (Speck 1964, 129–30). This ancient fear of the dead can still be observed in parts of northeastern Mexico where contact with corpses is thought by the Huastec Maya to result in malignant forms of cancer (Alcorn 1984, 224).

Among the eastern Cherokee "groin pain" was often associated with physical contact with the dead. The antidote, recorded in the unpublished field notes of Frans Olbrechts, was a plant whose botanical name remains obscure but which was known by the Cherokee of the nineteenth century as gho:la ('bone') gv:dhlí:sgi ('it that is able to splice it') (Kilpatrick and Kilpatrick, "Eastern Cherokee Ethnobotany," n.d.).

According to Swanton, the aboriginal Cherokee and Natchez also subscribed to the belief that the eating utensils belonging to the deceased were polluted. If someone violated this taboo and ate off a tainted dish, they would suffer episodes of acute stomach pain and nausea (Swanton 1928, 669).

Even among modern Cherokee communities in Oklahoma, a residue of this ancient fear exists about the contaminating effects of human remains. One Cherokee-Natchez medicine man warned that when building a house one must be eternally vigilant about the materials used because "blocks of sand and gravel may contain the disintegrated bodies of the dead. Even new lumber may be impregnated with the blood of the dead" (Tse:gi Ganv:hnawó:i field notes n.d.).

Cherokee apprehensions about the defiling potency of groundup human remains can probably be traced to folk beliefs about witchcraft. Among the Navajo and the Apache "corpse poison," a granulated powder extracted from plundered graves in cemeteries, is recognized as a primary ingredient that witches and sorcerers use to spread their evil (Kluckhohn 1944, 25; and Basso 1969, 34).

Besides these sources of contamination, it was generally held that, under certain conditions, the magical powers of a folk healer could be "spoiled" or "turned back" by a variety of causes. Here, however, the failure of a therapeutic regime does not seem to be linked in the Cherokee mind to a patient's failure to respond to a set of cultural symbols, as Finkler noted in her study of Mexican Spiritualist temples (1983), but to the capacious nature of paranormal energy itself.

To be an effective conduit of supernatural power a folk healer must maintain a balance between magic and medicine. The misuse of magic is thought to affect one's natural healing abilities: "If a doctor is doing evil conjuring, his good medicine will fail to work" (Tse:gi Ganv: hnawó:i field notes n.d.).

To safeguard their arcane abilities from pollution Cherokee medicine men, traditionally, had to assume a modest attitude about their paranormal talents and to avoid public boasting. As one well-respected traditionalist put it, "Long ago a medicine man, when approached, used to say: 'I'll doctor you a little bit.' To get help from Above, he had to be humble" (Tse:gi Ganv:hnawó:i field notes n.d.).

Exposure to an "impure" environment, such as the presence of a sick person, can "close the door" or seriously contaminate one's capacity to cure. To counteract this situation a medicine man might safeguard his magical potency by chewing a sassafras root, then, mixing it with his own saliva, rub the substance on his face and on his hands (Tse:gi Ganv:hnawó:i field notes n.d.).

One prominent Cherokee medicine man used to drink sassafras tea after visiting his patients at a local government hospital. Sometimes, this same individual would give his patients a white cloth bag containing sassafras roots to wear around their necks. This procedure was thought to help the bedridden keep their vital energies intact (Tse:gi Ganv:hnawó:i field notes n.d.).

After the death of a patient, a medicine man was considered ritually "unclean." It was believed that he must avoid seeing his clients for four days (Tse:gi Ganv:hnawó:i field notes n.d.).

To regenerate his curative powers a Cherokee medicine man was required to "Go to the Water" and ritually vomit for four mornings during each cycle of the new moon. To accomplish this cleansing, the medicine man rose early in the morning and ingested a mildly toxic root. Then he walked to the bank of a stream and dug a sloping hole close to the flowing water so that the liquid seeped into and filled the depression. Next, to empower this purgative act the medicine man recited a formula, blew over the water in the excavated hole, scooped a drink from it, and then regurgitated into the cavity. To safeguard himself from further spiritual/physical pollution the folk healer then covered up his work before departing the scene (Tse:gi Ganv:hnawó:i field notes n.d.).

Mindful of the vulnerability of their powers to contamination, the Cherokee folk healers also "renewed" their magical formulae every seven months to maintain their potency. Usually, this involved a "Going to the Water" ritual as well (Tse:gi Ganv:hnawó:i field notes n.d.).

Text 31 "Going to the Water"

Caption

dighahnawadv:sdi	*niga:di*	*gahl(i)gwo:gi*
law	all	seven

hnanila:sda'lv	*dego:tsalv v:sga*
clans	it includes them

gohú:sdi	*tsuni:gh(a)dhilé:gi*
something	which one attacks

dale:hnido:hv	*yí:gi*	*ale*	*da:dhliyv:sv*
arisen, he	if it is	or	grappling them, one

yí:gi   *na:sgi*   *gayv:na:i*   *iyu:nal(i)sdoˀdí:yi*
if it is   that   walking on, they   to become, they

yan(a)dan(v)dhelidó:ha   *yida:nada:gh(a)dhilé:ga*
if they think   if they attack

unu:svgwo   *na:sgi*   *un(v)dahni:ya:sdi*
themselves   that   to flee, they

u:n(a)dodhlv́:sv   *yí:gi*   *digu:dalé:sdi*
formed, they   if it is   to free them, it

ugv:wahli   *ale*   *iyú:n(a)sdi*
for the purpose of   and   the kind, they

du:n(a)dhliyv:sv   3ne
grappling them, they   third

gahl(i)gwo:gi   *iga:hl(a)sdaˀla:gi*   *ge:sv*   *ani:yá:v*
seven   clans   being, it   within, they

un(a)do:tsalé:dv   *degv:wani:gh(a)dhile:gv*
detached, they   they attacked them

yí:gi   *na:hna*   *do:dile:hv:sgv*
if it is   there   arising, he

na:sgi   *u:gitsí:sgi*   *ama:yi*
that   dawn   water place

atsv́:sdi   4ne
to go and return, one   fourth

tsigohew:la   *na:sgi*   *g(v)dho:dhi*   *tso:lagayv́:li*
which written, it   that   to use, one   tobacco, old

Free Translation

The law includes all of the Seven Clans. If someone attacks them or struggles against them or if they are traveling and think they might be

ambushed, this is for the purpose of freeing them from all three kinds of
strife. Within the Seven Clans if they are attacked separately, then at
dawn they are to go and return to a water place four times. It is written
that one should use "remade" tobacco.

Spell

ka!	*sge!*	*na:gwo*	*nv:no:hi*	*ada:nvnigá*
ka!	listen!	now	path-place	it has come to lie down

na:gwo	*ahnu:wo:gi*	*uné:gv*	*ganv:tsiga*
now	the cloth	white	it fell down

na:gwo	*igvnagata*		*uné:ga*	*na:gwo*
now	odors that we have brought		white	now

ahigale:yedv	*adv:ni:ga*	7
scatter it	he has come to say	[seven]

yv:wi	*ganv:hí:dv*	*tsa:hlidho:hi:sdi*
person	long, he	repose, you

gohú:sdi	*hali:sdisgi*	*nige:sv́:na*
something	can overpower, you	never

na:gwo	*agwada:nvdhogí*	*doda:sgwale:hiʔsoʔda:ne:li*	*dasgwo:dhlv́hisáne:li*
now	my soul	you are going to raise	you are going to renew for me

ha	*na:gwo*	*deda:sgwale:hiʔsoʔda:neli:gá*
ha	now	you have just come to raise it

yv:wi	*ganv:hí:dv*
person	long, he

agwada:nvdhogí	*gagila:wisoga*
soul, my ·	I have come carrying

yv:wi	*ganv:hí:dv*
person	long, he

dikahna:wadΰdv   *tsadv:ne:li:gá*
the decree   you have come to pronounce

igv:yiyu   *di:galΰ:la²diyΰ:i*
first, very   heavens

ha tsu:sΰ:hidv   *tsane:hlanΰ:hi*
ha! all-night   you provider

gayé:gwo:ni   *uyo:lotsi:hluhí*
July   it fell short

dikahna:wadΰdv   *ghwado²nvdi:se:sdi*
the decree   he will be able to do it.

ha   *gohΰ:sdi*   *halísdisgí*   *nige:sΰ:na*
ha!   something   can overpower you   never

dikahna:wadΰdv   *ghwado²di:se:sdi*
the decree   he will be able to do it

dha²line   *di:galΰ:la²diyí*   *iyv:dv*
second   heavens   farther on

agwada:nvdhogí   *gagila:wlsogá*
my soul   I have come carrying

yv:wi   *ganv:hí:dv*
person   long, he

dikahna:wadΰdv   *tsadv:ne:li:gá*
the decree   you have come to pronounce

ga²lo²hni   *de:gvwado:v*   *tsu:sΰ:hidv*   *tsane:hlanΰ:hi*   *uyo:lotsi:hlvhí*
August   named   all-night   provider, you   it fell short

agwada:nvdhogí   *gagihla:wisoga*
soul, my   I have come carrying

yv:wi   ganv:hídv
person   long, he

dikahna:wadúdv   ha   ghwado?nvdi:se:sdi
the decree   ha   he will be able to do it

tso?í:ne   di:galú:la?diyi:i   iyv:dv
third   heavens   over there

(dulisdi)   di:gwadú:dv   usv:hidv
September   named   let him rest

une:hlanú:hi   ha   uyo:lotsi:hlvhi
the one who provides   ha   it fell short

agwada:nvdogí   gagila:wisogá
soul, my   I have come carrying

yv:wi   ganv:hí:dv
person   long, he

dikana:wadúdv   ha   gvwado?nvdi:se:sdi
the decree   ha   he will be able to do it

ha   gohú:sdi   niga:hlisdi:sgi   nige:sú:na
ha   something   then it will be happening, it   never

nv:gine   digalúla?diyú   iyv:dv
fourth   heavens   several

agwada:nvdhogí   gagila:wisoga
soul, my   I have come carrying

(du:ni:nodhi)   de:gvwadó:dv
October   named

ha   tsu:sú:hidv   tsane:hlanú:hi   uyo:lotsi:hlvhi
ha   all-night   provider, you   it fell short

agwada:nvdhogí *gagila:wisogá*
soul, my   I have come carrying

[Here the text omits the refrain concerning the fifth month, November.]

yv:wi *ganv:hí:dv*
person long, he

dikahna:wadv́dv *ha* *gvwado'nvdi:se:sdí*
the decree   ha he will be able to do it

[suda]liné *di:galv́:la'diyí* *iyv:da*
sixth   heavens   over there

agwada:nvdhogí *gagila:wisogá*
soul, my   I have come carrying

(usgi:yi) *de:gvwadó:dv*
December named

tsu:sv́:hidv *tsane:hlanv́:hi* *uyo:lotsi:hlvhí*
all-night   you provider it fell short

agwada:nvdhogí *gagila:wisogá*
soul, my   I have come carrying

yv:wi *ganv:hí:dv*
person long

dikahna:wadv́dv *ha* *gvwado'nvdi:se:sdí*
the decree   ha he will be able to do it

ha *gohú:sdi* *halísdisgí*   *nige:sv́:na*
ha something can overpower you never

dikahna:wadv́dv *ha* *gvwado'nvdi:se:sdí*
the decree   ha he will be able to do it

7   *di:galv́:la²diyí:i* *iyv:da*
seventh heavens   farther on

agwada:nvdhogí *gagila:wisogá*
soul, my   I have come carrying

unolv
January

na:gwo *dvda:sgwale:hisodá:neli*
now   you are going to elevate it

sge *tsane:hlanv́:hi* *a²hnigwo*
listen provider, you right here

u:lidátlv *tsaltóhisti*   *na:gwo*
beyond you are calling exultantly now

gohú:sdi *tsanú:hlidi* *nige:sv́:na na:gwo*
something you fail   being, not now

agwada:nvdhogí *dasqwo:tlvhisanelí* *doda:sgwale:hisoda:neli*
soul, my   you will descend you are going to elevate it

dasqwo:tlvhisanelí *ado:lanv́:sdi* *gvwadv:dí*
you will descend walking stick he will use

adolanv́:sdi *uné:gv* *gvwalv:galo:hisdi* *nitsv:ndisesdí*
walking stick white at a slant   the way you will be
                   holding it

tsane:hlanv́:hi *a²hni* *e:la²dí* *na:gwo* *agwada:nvdhogí*
provider, you here below now soul, my

tsiga:so:dhani:gá   *adv́*
I have just come to breathe upon it he said

tsustadógi *tsidóhisdani:gá*
I stand here I have just come to prolong it

galú:laˀdi   *no:ghwisi*   *wásudó*
above   stars   peep out

tsatlv:ghwodiyú   *na:gwo*
he loves greatly   now

dikahna:wadúdv   *tsadv:neli:gá*
the decree   you have just come to pronounce

agwada:nvdhogí   *tsiga:so:dhani:gá*
soul, my   I have just come to breathe upon it

adagwo   *advwa:satiyésgv*
the forest here   it is swaying

iyv:dv   *tsalv:dohésdi*
farther   you are calling exultantly

dhlv:datsi   *tsatlv́ghwodiyú*
panther   he loves greatly

dikahna:wadúdv   *ha*   *gvwadvˀnvdi:se:sdi*
the edict   ha   he will be able to fullfil it

hida:we:hiyu   *u:lidadlv:qwó*   *dighádhane:da*   *tsadv:nehesdí*
wizard, you, much   beyond, just   he sees   you will be doing

yv:wi   *ganv:hí:dv*
person   long, he

tsalv:dohésdi   *hiyehla:istvgwo*
you are calling exultantly   you come by calling exultantly

agí:nv   *nagí*
young   he is

tsiga:so:dhani:gá   *na:gwo*
I have just come to breathe upon it   now

agwada:nadhogí	*doda:sgwale:hiˀsoˀda:ne:li*	*hi:nesdi*	*ge:sʋˀ*
soul, my	you are going to elevate it	your breast	it is

dota:lehisani
you will stand again

(diqwadóidú)*	*(digiyʋ:wi)**
(named, I)	(people, they, my)

[*The appropriate name and clan of the client are inserted.]

Free Translation

Now, listen! Now the road has just come to lie at your feet. Now the White Cloth has just fallen down. Now the white perfumes have been brought. "Now, scatter them!" he has just come to say. (Seven Times.)

Long Person, you are in repose. Nothing can overpower you.

Now you are going to elevate my soul. You are going to renew it. Ha! Now you have just come to elevate it. Long Person, I have just come bearing my soul.

Long Person, you have just come to pronounce the Edict: "Ha! Take your rest in the First Heaven (July)."

You Maker, it was too confining. He will be able to fulfill the Edict. Ha! Nothing can ever overpower you. He will be able to fulfill the Edict.

To the Second Heaven farther on I have come bearing my soul.

Long Person, you have just come to pronounce the Edict: "Take your rest through August." You maker, it was too confining.

Long Person, I have come bearing my soul.

Ha! He will be able to fulfill the Edict: "In the Third Heaven farther on, September, take your rest." Ha! Maker, it was too confining.

Long Person, I have come bearing my soul.

Ha! He will be able to fulfill the Edict. Ha! Nothing can ever overpower you.

To the Fourth Heaven farther on I have come bearing my soul.

"Ha! Through October take your rest." You Maker, it was too confining.

Long Person, I have come bearing my soul.

Ha! He will be able to fulfill the Edict.

To the Fifth Heaven farther on I have come bearing my soul.

"Take your rest through November." You Maker, it was too confining. Long Person, I have come bearing my soul.

Ha! He will be able to fulfill the Edict. Ha! Nothing can ever overpower you. Ha! He will be able to fulfill the Edict.

To the Sixth Heaven farther on I have come bearing my soul.

"Through December (it was too confining)—"take your rest." You Maker, Long Person, you have just come to pronounce the Edict.

To the Seventh Heaven farther on I have come bearing my soul. Now it has become part of a congregation there. Listen, you Maker, now you are going to renew my soul. Now you are going to elevate it.

Out beyond where I stand here you are calling exultantly. You can fail in nothing. Now you are going to renew my soul. You are going to elevate it. You are going to renew it.

He will use the White Walking Stick. You will be holding the White Walking Stick at a slant.

You maker, now my soul here below—

"I have just come to breathe upon it," he said. "I am standing here. I have just come to prolong it."

On high the stars are peeping out. He loves you deeply. Now you have just come to pronounce the Edict.

"My soul—"I have just come to breathe upon it."

Here the forest is swaying. Out beyond here, Panther, you are calling exultantly. He loves you deeply. The Edict—Ha! You will be able to fulfill it. You great Wizard! He sees what you will be doing just beyond. Long Person, you are calling exultantly. You come by calling exultantly. He is young.

"I have just come to breathe upon it."

"Now you are going to elevate my soul to your breast."

"You will stand again."

"My name is ____. My clan is ____."

Commentary

James Adair was probably correct in attributing fatalistic beliefs to the aboriginal Cherokees that he encountered: "For they affirm, that there is a fixt [sic] time, and place, when and where, everyone must die, without any possibility of averting it" (Adair [1775], 1930, 33). Despite this belief one finds little sense of pessimism in the highly poetic text above, which brims with ecstatic images of "renewed and elevated souls" and "white walking sticks" (an ethereal metaphor for old age).

As noted earlier, this beautiful and sonorous text was recited at daybreak while the subject to be cleansed stood at the edge of a flowing stream, facing the rising sun in the east. At the conclusion of the recitation, the patient underwent a symbolic immersion in the water, a laving repeated either four or seven times.

In "Going to the Water" rites, which have been employed to divine the longevity of a patient, folk healers often refer to a standardized framework of seven successive heavens to which the patient's soul may aspire to elevate itself:

> Each upper world represents a definite period of life, usually a year, sometimes a month. . . . Should the omens in the water be propitious up to the mention of the third, fourth, or fifth upper world, the client will live in peace three, four, or five years longer. If all goes well until he is raised up to the seventh or highest upper world he may expect at least a seven years' lease of life (Mooney and Olbrechts 1932, 234).

The manuscript presented here dates to about 1940. The calligraphy belongs to Dlanus Toyanisi, a medicine man who lived in Adair County, Oklahoma. My late father, who first made an unpublished transcription of this text, taking note of "its mesmeric reiterations, its dialogue-like shifts of person and its towering and touching climax," questioned whether this particular document had not served some larger purpose in Cherokee life:

> It does not appear to dovetail psychologically into any of the common circumstances of life motivating water rites. One senses in it the surge of some necessity national in size, above individual lives and their affairs. I wonder, in fact, if it does not owe its preservation in writing to the stirring days of World War Two when it may have been recalled from the faltering memory of a shaman and transcribed for use at some valedictory ceremony for Cherokee soldiers, destined for distant places.

Text 32   "For Going to the Water"

Caption

ama:yi	*didatsv́:sdi:sgini*
water place	to go and return, them

ahyv:dagwalo:sgi	*tsuno:gidv*
it which thunders	he had sung

ama:yi   *adawo:sdi*   *sunalé:i*
water place   one bathes   early morning

4   *tsu:sv:hidá*
four   overnights [days]

nidagatséhlv:na   *tsinigó:wane*   *yv:wi*
desired, one not   bothered   people

diná:doni:sgi
conjurors

[to be sung]

ohanadu   4
ohanadu!   [four times]

Spell

a:sgaya   *gigagé:i*   *u:yoi*   *tsósdadahnvtli*
man   red, he   wrong   "fellow brother"

tsadv:ne:i   *hiye:lv:ʔ*   *tsuhilodv*   *nuda:lesv*   *gv:sde:lí:di*   *tsadv:ne:i*
you said   your body   you have   everything   one to   you said
                cleansed   help it

a:sgaya   *de:hálu:géʔ*   *tsadv:ne:i*
man   purple   you said

a:sgaya   *tsane:ga*   *hide:we:hiyu*
man   white, you   wizard, you much

[one contemplates here]

a:sgaya   *dalo:ni*   *hida:we:hiyu*
man   yellow   wizard, you, much

ghaʔ sge: *ahyv:dagwalo:sgi*   *tsane:tsvhi*   *nuda:lesv*
now listen   it which thunders   you have decided   everything

gv:sde:lí:di   *gese:sdi*   *tsadv:ne:i*
one to help it   it will be   you said

gahligwo:gi   *igáhlisda:dale:gí*
seven   clan districts

ulisgé:dv   *unada:telidi*   *unanu:gosdi*   *nige:sv́:na*
intruder   in their midst   to come again   never

ha   *ehawí:ni*   *iyv:dv*   *hwidiganú:dosiga*
ha   deep   far   over there, have just sunk, they

tsuna:de:nvdhogi   *tsunanu:gosdi*   *nige:sv́:na*
souls, their   to appear, they   never

sa'gho:ni   *unadv́:nehesdi*
blue   they will be asking

ayv:sgini   *sa'gho:ni*   *agwa:dvdi*   *nige:sv́:na*
as for me   blue   will ask   never

ha   *yv:wi*   *ganv:hí:dv*
ha   person   long, he

tsalisdé:hlvdo'di   *gese:sdi*   *tsadv:ne:i*
to help one, you   it will be   you said

nvdó:hi:yadv   *dugitsv:nisesdi*   *tsadv:ne:i*
sun place, completely   day after day, it will be   you said

nvdó:hi:yadv   *dude:dhiyehi:se:sdi*
sun place   year after year, it will be

tlesdí   *agise:gogisvgi*   *ulisgé:dv*   *dinadá:tselvhi*
let it not   to overcome me   the intruder   agreed upon

tlesdí   *gvgisé:gogisvgi*   7
let it not   to overcome me   seven

sgwane:hlanv́:hi   *hu:dhlegi nv:do*
provider, my   uncover sun it, you

wudé:li:ga   *hwiqué:gahvga*
over there goes down, it   we have just come to place it elsewhere

Uyo   *anada:nvdhé:gi*
evil   those that think

hilv:hiyu   *nidatsa:gitahvsdi*   *nige:sv́:na*
ancient, very   will be turning you   never

ganesai   *digv:hnagé*   *dotsu:hlidho:hi:sdv*
boxes   black, they   reposing place, they

tsanudóhiseli:ga   *tsada:dhogi*   *hilv:hiyu*
you have just come to fall   soul, your   ancient,very

ditsaluhi:sdí   *nige:sv́:na*
to go and return   never

Free Translation

Thunder is sung [e.g., Ohanadu!] as one goes to a water place [a free-flowing stream]. At the water place, one bathes early in the morning for four days if one does not want to be bothered by conjurors.

[To be sung]
Ohanadu! Ohanadu! Ohanadu! Ohanadu!

[To be recited]
"Red Man, "Fellow Brother," you said.
"To help everything, you have cleansed
your body," you said.
"Purple Man," you said.
White Man, You Great Wizard!
(Pause to contemplate the condition of the patient.)

"Yellow Man, You Great Wizard!
Now! Listen! Thunder, you have decided everything!

You said that you would help it so that
the Disease in the midst of the Seven Clans would never come again!

Ha! Deep, Far Away! Over there, they have just sunk
their souls, never to reappear!
They will be asking for the Blue!
As for me, the Blue will never ask!

Ha! Long Person, you said that you will help me
to be completely in the Sun Place, day after day!
[Long Person], you said [that you will help me to be]
completely in the Sun Place, year after year!

Let not the specified illness overcome me.
Let it not overcome me!
Seven!
(Here, the reciter contemplates silently.)

My Provider, uncover it [the Illness]!
We have come to place it elsewhere
Over there, where the sun goes down!
Ancient One, those who think evil of me
will not be turning you [aside].

Ancient One,
the black boxes will be their resting place!
Your soul has just come to fall!
Never to return!

Commentary

The above "Going to the Water" text preserved in the Uwe:da:sadhi
Sa:wali papers is designed to counteract a conjuror's spell. The instructions, penciled in by my father (along with a musical sketch of the
refrain to be sung), are explicit about its intended audience: "This is
exclusively a *doctor's* medicine for *himself*. A layman cannot use this."
Folk healers stand east and sing the Ohanadu refrain and recite the text
the requisite four times. The magic is believed to be made stronger if
reciters then actually swim in the stream, rather than just dipping their
bodies in the water or splashing it over their heads four times. Evidence

of the formula's efficacy can be found in the comments of another Cherokee medicine man who added, "Good for *anything*, to help oneself."

Text 33 "To Divine with a Needle"

Gha?	*yv:wi*	*ganv:hí:dv*
Now!	person long,	he

gvyada:dolisda:neli:ga
I have just come to pray to you.

Wa-hya!	*Hi-na-du!*
Wa-hya!	Hi-na-du!

Gha?	*dasqwo:lihi:saneli*
Now!	will remake it, you

agwada:nvdho	*degvle:gwasi:sgesdi*	*deganvhi:gesdi*
soul, my	again, will rise, I	to last longer

Wa-hya!	*Hi-na-du!*
Wa-hya!	Hi-na-du!

hina:sane:siga		*ulisgé:dv*	*agwada:nvdho*
you have come to pull it away		intruder	soul, my

Free Translation

Now! Long Person!
I have just come to pray to you!
Wa-hya! hi-na-du! (sung four times)
Now! You will remake my soul!
Let my rising ups become longer!
Wa-hya! hi-na-du! (sung four times)
Let the disease be removed from my soul.

Commentary

This "Going to the Water" text designed to ascertain the medical condition of a patient was authored by the Cherokee folk healer Green

Waterdown. Because most natural afflictions such as sunburn, cuts, headaches, and so on, are treated by folk remedies, the etymology of illness sought here is, undoubtedly, of supernatural origin. Appended to this manuscript, which dates to about 1920, was a brief note in English that states that one is "to use a needle to look into a person's life."

Wa-hya ('wolf') is a symbolic reference to wizardry. As noted earlier in chapter 2, members of the wolf clan were noted for their special occult powers (Kilpatrick and Kilpatrick 1967b, 119). *Hi-na-du!* is the onomatopoeic sound for Thunder, the supernatural ally of the Cherokee.

Ul(i)sgé:dv, the Cherokee generic word for disease, was first translated by Mooney (1891) as 'intruder.' Modern Cherokee scholars, however, have insisted upon rendering the word as 'the important one.' In my estimation Mooney's earlier translation appears to capture the essence of the Cherokee medicinal ethos. Cherokee, like most indigenous languages, defines phenomena in highly spatial terms. Maladies, (particularly those of a supernatural origin), are considered to be transmitted from a distance, and victims are often "shot" by the malicious intentions of evil persons from a distance. This notion of illness as a "violater of social space" or "intruder," remains at the heart of the word.

In his study of the rituals of the Ndembu tribe of Zambia Victor Turner argued that divination and revelation had contrasting social functions. Divination was "specially concerned with uncovering the hidden causes of ills brought about by the immoral or self-serving thoughts, words, or deeds of individuals," whereas revelation "asserts the fundamental power and health of the society and nature grasped integrally" (Turner 1975, 15–16).

In the Cherokee context both of these social functions seem to be intertwined. Although "Going to the Water" rites might elucidate the etiology of personal disorders, they also serve as revelatory instruments that reaffirm the common values of purification for the whole community.

7

"On Being Conjured"

Explanations of Cherokee Witchcraft and Sorcery

I should preface this chapter with the disclaimer that in more than forty years of living with or close to Cherokees I have yet to meet a single witch or anyone who claimed to be one. I cannot make the same statement about conjurors, however, as the following case history demonstrates.

Case 1: E. N.

In the mid-1970s, a full decade after the last of these texts was written, a close relative of mine was reputedly "conjured" to death. For the record, E. N. was a healthy full-blood Cherokee woman in her mid-fifties who lived in northeastern Oklahoma. Having earned her master's degree in education, E. N. seemed to be quite accustomed to living in both the Indian and the white worlds.

One year before her death she decided to break off a longstanding relationship with another full-blood, "Mike," and to marry a wealthy, Caucasian real estate developer. A few months after her engagement this woman, who had been perfectly healthy, came down with a life-threatening case of multiple myeloma (cancer of the bone marrow).

When this fact was discovered, her sisters warned the patient that her old boyfriend had paid a *dida:hnese:sgi* to make her ill and that she should consult with an Indian doctor immediately. Her new husband, however, not attuned to such "backward" and "ignorant" practices, decided to send her for modern medical treatment to M. D. Anderson, a renowned cancer research facility in Houston, Texas. Unfortunately, despite a regime of chemotherapy, experimental drugs, and the attention of world-class physicians, E. N. expired within one year of her diagnosis.

I had the opportunity to visit E. N. in the hospital shortly before her

121

death. On that occasion she told me about an incident that convinced her that she had been conjured. One afternoon, while lying in her hospital bed, she awoke to find an old Indian fellow, wearing a white cowboy hat, sitting at the edge of her bed. From his strange stare E. N. instantly recognized this person as the conjuror, "Walker." Shocked by Walker's intrusion into her private room, she ordered him to leave, and "he vanished."

There is an interesting postscript to this story. E. N.'s funeral was held one cold, blustery day in December in Oklahoma City. I had flown there from Los Angeles to attend the service. After the ceremony, my brother and I decided to drive back to Tahlequah, where he lived. Along the way we stopped off at a truck stop diner near Tulsa to eat.

In a twist of Jungian synchronicity the first person we met in the diner was "Mike," E. N.'s old boyfriend, who invited us to join him. Sharing the table with "Mike" was an older gentleman who wore a white cowboy hat.

As we sat down, "Mike" introduced us to "Walker," and we shook hands with the reputed conjuror. In a round of small talk we all commiserated about the tragic loss of my relative. Because I held E. N. in great affection, I attempted to keep my fugitive emotions from these alleged conspirators.

Then "Mike" asked me in a low-key tone, "What are you going to do now?" The question, at first, seemed normal under the circumstances. I sensed, however, that a veiled threat lurked behind this subterfuge of polite concern, particularly, because Walker's "strange eyes" scrutinzed me, probing my heart for vengeful schemes.

Taught in true Cherokee fashion not to "give offence" or to "make a scene," especially in front of strangers, I answered simply that I planned to return home to Los Angeles. Then, perhaps to bring some sense of closure to this whole affair, I heard myself say, "So it's over now, isn't it?"

In proper Cherokee fashion an agreement was reached. Heads nodded; hands were shaken. Because the matter was now officially closed, my brother and I then moved to another table. My interview with the notorious Cherokee conjuror had ended.

I realize that this case history, extracted from my youth, falls short of the empirical ideal of being "carefully observed . . . with a modicum of control . . . quantitative, hard, and systematic" stressed by some anthropologists (Nutini and Roberts 1993, 4). I bring this ethnographic data to the reader's attention, however, not because I wish to sensationalize the facts but because this case demonstrates one salient point: even though Cherokee culture has undergone centuries of social transformation brought on by exposure to the technological advances that characterize the modern era, witches and sorcerers remain, in some form, a vital ontological reality to my mother's people.

Although the present set of texts are informative about the spoken words and the physical procedures used traditionally by Cherokee folk healers to actualize magic, they do not explain why these ancient beliefs in the supernatural have persisted, even today, among the Cherokee people. Thus, one cannot leave the subject without attempting to postulate some plausible explanation about why the belief in witches and sorcerers remains so remarkably intact in present-day Cherokee communities.

To begin such an analysis it should be emphasized at the onset that most modern anthropologists have long discarded Levy Bruhl's assertion that the "primitive" mentalities of preliterite societies operate in a purely mystical fashion (cf. Morris 1987, 183–86). Instead, most anthropologists today would argue that the "mysticism" observed in nonwestern tribal societies exhibits its own inherent inner logic and that this "logic" can be discovered through careful ethnographic reconstruction. Nutini and Roberts (1993) cogently stress this point: "There is every indication that, even under the influence of the strongest and most pervasive witchcraft, sorcery, or any other magical complex, most actors in a social system behave and act most of the time, situationally and contextually, in a common-sense fashion and according to the dictates of 'natural' law" (Nutini and Roberts 1993, 14). Mindful that many of the theoretical frameworks developed by anthropologists since the formative research of Evans-Pritchard ([1937] 1976) and Kluckhohn (1944) are not wholly adequate to explain the range of mystical or "irrational" behavior associated with the practice of witchcraft and sorcery in all human societies, I bring here a multidisciplinary approach to my analysis of the phenomenon of supernaturalism among the Cherokee, one which incorporates historical, sociopsychological, and ideological perspectives as well.

Functionalism

No body of theory has been so widely used by anthropologists to explain the witchcraft-sorcerer dynamic as functionalism, first postulated by Evans-Pritchard ([1937] 1976) and later elaborated by Clyde Kluckhohn (1944). The underlying concept of functionalism is that all human societies seek psychic equalibrium or integration through the application of various adjustive or adaptive methods.

Evans-Pritchard's most notable contribution to functionalism was to argue that the witchcraft-sorcerer complex offers its believers an explanatory framework for unexpected outbreaks of disease or bouts of personal misfortune. It has long been observed that witches exercise occult powers that "cannot be detected so that the cause can only be recognized when the damage comes to light" (Mair 1969, 7).

One classic aspect of the witch (discussed in Middleton 1963, 262) is its incarnation as the ever-invisible "creature of the night" (e.g., Raven Mocker and Night Walker). It is the presence of this unknown predator, this almost uncontrollable force that precipitates the calamity and death that drives human beings to "put a name to their anxieties" (Mair 1969, 199). This ever-present, lurking specter of evil rejects the cultural values of society and lives outside the human community. As a result, tribal members feel free to "discharge their aggression on the imaginary person whom it is 'proper to fear and hate'" (Mair 1969, 200).

A side effect of this model of the "night witch," the unseen entity, is that it fuels high levels of suspicion in folk societies. Because no one can pinpoint the real source of trouble, harm may come from "distant, impersonal figures or they may be members of the victim's community or even his own kin-group" (Walker 1989, 3). Shimony comments on a similar attitude prevalent on the Iroquois reserve: "Everybody feels himself to be a potential victim of a witch and one cannot foretell which particular attribute will excite the envy of the evil-doer" (Shimony 1989, 148).

Historically, among the western Cherokee, suspicion of witchcraft appears to have permeated all social classes irrespective of age or gender. Washburn, a missionary to the Arkansas band of the Cherokee, writes:

> They considered these beings as not only possessing an individual existence and capable of assuming a visible form; but also, as often taking up their abode in men, women, and children. This last they could not do without the consent of the individual, but any person, whenever he or she might choose, could become the residence of one of these malignant demons (Washburn [1869] 1971, 133).

In one aspect this far-reaching hysteria seems socially disruptive. The belief in witchcraft can serve a vital function, however, by providing a theory of causation, as Kluckhohn once noted, because the failures of a conjuror to cure a patient can be blamed on "the interference of witch-craft rather than to its inherent inadequacy" (Mair 1969, 201).

According to proponents of functionalism, another way in which the witchcraft-sorcery complex contributes to the stabilization of tribal societies is by offering a mode of moral instruction. All human societies share the same fundamental philosophical problem of explaining and articulating the existence of good and evil. Proclaiming the existence of witches "affirms solidarity" among a tribal group because it allows this ideological paradox to be understood in a vivid, unequivocal manner by "dramatically defining what is bad" (Mair 1969, 201).

The second aspect of the witch is particularly apt here because it represents the model of the "unneighborly person" (discussed in M. Wilson 1957, 14) described as "the one whom one would not wish to resemble and also the one whom one should avoid offending" (Mair 1969, 202). This more tangible "unneighborly person" "behaves badly in the accepted cultural context," and the resultant actions represent a failure of meeting specific social obligations (Wilson 1957, 14). It is this form of witch (or conjuror) who figures most prominently in Kluck-hohn's analysis as either the victim of scapegoatism or as the perpetrator of criminal acts whose prosecution reaffirms the moral order of that society.

According to Kluckhohn (who stressed the psychological effects of supernaturalism), witchcraft works as a kind of dual-edged sword. On one hand, it "provides identity for culturally dissatisfied individuals: the alienated and displaced, and those who do not easily fit into the established norm of the society" while, on the other, it helps those individuals who uphold "mainstream" values by allowing them to express "hostilities in socially acceptable ways, thereby relieving psychological tensions" (Nutini and Roberts 1993, 20).

It should be stressed here that the psychological tensions experienced by folk societies who subscribe to such supernatural beliefs appear to be culturally bound, grounded in the ethical norms of the group. Walker (1989) notes that these "conventional, culturally patterned fears and frustations" can vary widely for "in Tecospa and Tepepan they are heavily sexual, whereas among the Iroquois, they relate more to economic frustration. Among the Nez Perce and Pueblo they often reflect health anxieties" (Walker 1989, 4).

The disquietude and consternation that Cherokees feel about witches and sorcerers as aggressive and hostile supernatural forces seem to emanate from their ethical worldview (cf. Fogelson 1975, 126). Among enclaves of traditional Cherokees the first cosmic principle of correct human behavior centers around what the late anthropologist Robert Thomas called "the harmony ideal." Among conservative Cherokees scrupulous attention must be given to maintaining "harmonious interpersonal relationships . . . by avoiding giving offense or the negative side, and by giving of himself to his fellow Cherokee in regard to his time and his material goods on the positive side" (Thomas 1958).

This synthesis of "harmony, balance, order, and sharing" serves not only on the level of a personal code but, according to one historian, expresses the "key values of the Cherokee religious ethic" (McLoughlin 1984, 18). According to Thomas, the Cherokee used their public ceremonies not only to promote "good feeling among the people" but also to demonstrate through ritual expression that "harmony and balance ensures and refurbishes the social, spiritual, and physical health of the people" (Thomas, personal correspondence, 1974).

During the nineteenth century this harmony ideal found expression in the *gadugi*, small economic cooperatives of Cherokee men who hired out their labor to neighboring farms and split the profits. "Poor aid" societies also existed that could be enlisted to clean graveyards, dig graves, and help families in financial straits to plant and harvest crops (Gilbert 1943, 213).

A corollary to the Cherokee "harmony" ideal is that "direct, open conflict is injurious to reputation" (Gearing 1962, 31). This ethic, which forbids "open face-to-face clashes," can be superseded by resorting to indirect means of attack—harmful gossip or conjuring—which work, in effect, as "weapons used by clashing wills which yet avoid face-to-face confrontation and the disallowed conflict" (Gearing 1962, 31).

Despite an avowed adherence to this harmonious ideal of psychological balance and social egalitarianism, Cherokee society, particularly during the nineteenth century, appears to have been caught up in endless blood feuds and witch killings which were, no doubt, precipitated by personal jealousies and ideological conflicts. Certainly, failure to fulfill this specified code of moral obligation must have cast many Cherokees into a suspicious light.

This was clearly the case with "Lucy," one of my relatives who lived during the early part of this century. Common gossip had it that "Lucy," half-sister of my grandmother, was a "witch." The accusations made against her were bolstered by "Lucy's" suspicious life style. She lived alone in the woods, never married, and was considered an "outsider" by the family. From the perspective of the traditional Cherokee ethical system, "Lucy" was suspect largely because she fit the classic mold of the "unneighborly person." Fortunately, even though she remained the subject of much malicious gossip during her life, "Lucy" was never, to my knowledge, publicly confronted about her secret motives. Had she lived a few decades earlier, she might easily have been put to death.

One of Kluckhohn's most powerful theoretical insights was that during periods of great social instability and popular unrest witchcraft and sorcery provide a viable "substitute outlet" for individual hostilities, especially when entrenched moral prohibitions forbid internal group conflict or aggression. As a result, during these volatile periods of sociopolitical turmoil one expects an increase in the volume of witchcraft accusations. If one examines the ethnohistorical record among the Cherokee, Kluckhohn's thesis receives strong evidential support.

Most historians focus on the psychic trauma brought upon the Cherokee people by their forced removal from their eastern homelands on the Trail of Tears in 1838. From the perspective of public concern and hysteria over witchcraft, however, the first quarter of the nineteenth century (a time when traditional values were being challenged by the evangelical efforts of missionaries) seems to have been a singularly difficult sociopsychological period for the Cherokee Nation.

One of the most compelling commentaries about the pervasiveness of Cherokee fears and anxieties over witches comes from the nineteenth-century missionary Cephas Washburn. Washburn, writing in 1822, describes the witch phobia suffered by one of his charges, an eleven-year-old Cherokee girl, Jane Hicks:

> The first convert was a little girl. . . . She had suffered much from superstitious fears, she was especially afraid of witches. As this was very common . . . one day, at the opening of school, I read a portion of Scripture, in which was some mention of witches. . . . She looked at me with a countenance of terror, as though she expected that one of these mysterious beings would seize upon me. . . . She laid aside her book and could not attend to her lesson, so deeply was this superstitious belief inwrought in the very depths of her soul. (Washburn [1869] 1971, 124–25)

Washburn's narrative graphically demonstrates that as of 1822 beliefs in the magical powers of witches were not only vibrant but were endemic to whole Cherokee communities, permeating down to its youngest members. In this highly charged atmosphere of fear and suspicion the wanton murder of suspected witches reached alarming proportions.

In 1812 a Cherokee woman told the eastern missionaries working at Brainerd Mission that all of her relations had been charged with witchcraft and summarily put to death. She, herself, was spared that fate because she was pregnant (Brainerd Journal, May 22, 1822, cited in McLoughlin 1986, 335).

In a pathetic anecdote Cephas Washburn describes how a Cherokee farmer, who had kindly raised his brother's five children after they were orphaned, was brutally murdered one day by his own nephew near Dwight Mission. The nephew, it turned out, had become convinced, through a third party, that the uncle was a witch and had been responsible for the untimely death of the other four children (the children had actually died of complications brought on by typhoid fever). The martyred uncle was later found to be innocent of the suspected crime.

According to Washburn, this ghastly crime was fairly typical of the social climate of the period. On the frailest of pretexts Cherokees were being victimized by their own kin: "Did anyone hold a grudge against his neighbor, he needed only to fix upon him the reputation of being a witch. His death was certain" (Washburn [1869] 1971, 138).

In 1826 Elias Boudinot, the full-blood Cherokee classical scholar and editor of the newspaper, *The Cherokee Phoenix*, published his pamphlet, "An Address to the Whites." The purpose of Boudinot's tract was to publicize recent advances that the Cherokee people had made, largely under the civilizing influences of Christianity. In his litany of Cherokee accomplishments Boudinot cited the fact that "the practice of putting aged persons to death for witchcraft" had been abolished (Perdue 1983, 75). Boudinot was, perhaps, referring to the passage of legislation by the Arkansas Cherokee Council in 1824, which had outlawed the killing of suspected witches. Whatever his source, the fact that such laws had to be passed in the first place speaks volumes about the extent of social unrest and the breakdown of customs during the early nineteenth century.

Intriguingly, this period of public vigilantism coincides with the decline of the conjuror's political power in Cherokee society. I use the term *conjuror* here to encompass the range of full-blood practitioners in folk healing and magic. Before the early nineteenth century, the conjuror had enjoyed an almost exalted status, particularly among Cherokee groups living in the eastern part of the United States.

Besides officiating over "sacred fire" ceremonies, conjurors were in charge of controlling the weather and divining when it was most beneficial for the community to plant and harvest crops (Gearing 1962, 28).

Conjurors also served as counselors to the ruling chiefs at every council meeting, often adorned in anthropomorphic gear to ward off evil spirits (Woodward 1963, 43,49). Conjurors also presided over the stickball competitions held between different villages and attempted, through their magic, to influence the outcome of the game (Fogelson 1971; A. Kilpatrick n.d.).

During the precolonial period Cherokee conjurors, in their archetypal role of priests, stood atop a tightly integrated social pyramid. This aboriginal Cherokee community was regulated by "formalized patterns of authority" (e.g., public ceremonies and rituals), and this high level of social integration was "symbolized by the centrally located townhouse and dance grounds . . . the community-supported priesthood and the common storehouse used during the festival season" (Holzinger 1961, 231–32).

Much of the prestige bestowed upon the Cherokee conjuror can be traced to the ancient myth surrounding the ritual murder of the monster, Stone-Clad, by a medicine man (Mooney 1900, 319). According to the myth, Stone-Clad, a voracious enemy of hunters, was rendered helpless by seven menstrual women who had been told by a medicine man to position themselves along his path. Weakened by his exposure to these "unclean" women, Stone-Clad was finally pinned to the earth by the medicine man, who drove seven sourwood stakes through him. Stone-Clad, who was also a conjuror, was then set ablaze by the angry and vengeful villagers. In an act of penitence the monster, on his funeral pyre, divulged his store of secret knowledge by singing aloud the sacred chants until he expired.

No doubt, Cherokee audiences could appreciate the cosmological implications of the story. Purification, (always an obsessive rite among the aboriginal Cherokee as evidenced by the formidable amount of "Going to the Water" texts) registers as a strong element here. This man-eating monster, who operates outside the moral community of humans, is brought under control by the polluting force of "unclean" women. Then Stone-Clad (and his secret powers) are consecrated and "re-purified" by the cleansing action of the ancient fire.

The role of the medicine man in this story is instructive because it is he who plots the overthrow of the monster and secures the creature for the sacrifice. The ritual killing of Stone-Clad transforms a dangerous presence into a benign source of transformational knowledge.

Although this myth provides a rationale for the conveyance of political power to the conjuror, it also reveals certain contradictory Cherokee attitudes about power and equality. The myth celebrates the egalitarian gesture of Stone-Clad, who deems to make public his knowledge of the sacred songs. In reality, though, traditional Cherokees adhere strongly to the notion that sacred wisdom and magical skills are not to be disseminated widely among the uninitiated.

The retelling of myths such as the conquest of Stone-Clad, no doubt, perpetuated the belief among the aboriginal Cherokees that their conjurors were, more or less, invincible because they derived their powers from such primordial events. This public confidence in the efficacy of their folk healers continued until the early eighteenth century when the first devastating outbreaks of smallpox occurred in 1738–39. According to Adair ([1775] 1930), many of the Cherokee conjurors were unable to cope with the spread of this epidemic and, as a gesture of defeat, burned their ritual equipment.

No conjuror, however gifted, could have foreseen the height of human tragedy that the Cherokee culture suffered during the eighteenth century. The advent of the missionaries, the forced removal of the tribe to Indian Territory, the outbreak of the Civil War, and, finally, the passage of the Dawes Act in 1887 all contributed to the psychic disintegration of these people. As a result, this whole period is marked by political fractionalism and social turmoil (cf. Reid 1970).

In Oklahoma during the 1870s and 1880s a critical economic schism developed in the Cherokee Nation between progressive mixed-blood Cherokees, who were either wealthy landowners or acculturated professionals, and the conservative full-bloods who were, for the most part, poor subsistence farmers (Champagne 1992, 210–11).

This cultural schism was further perpetuated around Tahlequah, Oklahoma (capital of the Cherokee Nation), when male and female seminaries were established in 1851. Here, the gentrified offspring of the new elite, the so-called flowers of the Cherokee, could pursue their white education at the expense of their native past (Mihesuah 1993, 30).

During this turbulent, postremoval period of the late nineteenth century, the conjuror, who had once been such an integral part of Cherokee ceremonial life, became divested of his public functions. As the Cherokee Nation was being dismantled around them, many conjurors found solace and fellowship by joining the Nighthawk Society, a branch of the Keetoowah organization. Chartered in 1858, the Keetoowah Society was established to create a bulwark against this increasing social change and to cultivate, as James Mooney suggested, "national feelings among the fullbloods in opposition to the innovating tendencies of mixed-blood elements" (McLoughlin 1994, 221). The conservative membership of the Keetoowahs was also dedicated to preserving the traditional values and rituals of their forefathers, particularly the maintenance of the "ancient fire" ceremonies, the stomp dance, and an enduring belief in the efficacy of the old magic.

It is, perhaps, no accident, then, that most of the nineteenth-century formulae reproduced in this book can be dated to this postremoval period in Oklahoma. Nor is it any surprise that most of the authors were full-fledged members of this nativistic organization.

In my view the upsurge in witch killings experienced in the nineteenth century seems motivated not only by the high degree of social unrest (as Kluckhohn postulated in his functionalism model) but also by the deterioration of the conjuror's traditional role in Cherokee society. It should be remembered that, historically, one of the conjurors' most highly regarded attributes was their ability magically to kill a witch and restore health to the patient or to the village.

During the nineteenth century the conjurors' skills were brought into serious question not only by the missionary but also by their own kin, for it must have been apparent to many Cherokees that the conjuror could no longer ward off the evil spirits who were bent on destroying this Indian Nation. During this troublesome period it is not surprising that the ordinary people, in an effort to restore some sense of order to their lives, usurped the legendary powers of the conjuror and took on the daunting task of witch killing themselves.

Viewed from this historical perspective, it is also clear now why so many Cherokee conjurors gravitated toward Christianity around the turn of the twentieth century. By becoming baptized and joining the church Cherokee conjurors were aligning themselves with the very forces that had once persecuted them.

This careful reconfiguration of the symbolic order, although not on the same level that John Watanabe has observed in his insightful study of the Mam-speaking Maya in Guatemala (Watanabe 1990), has, over decades, resulted in the same net effect. This nominal acceptance of the Christian faith has allowed the Cherokee conjurors to regain social visibility and spiritual credibility among their kinfolk and has served as the most expedient means to regain their lost social status.

The twentieth century has witnessed a remarkable demonstration of the survival skills of the Cherokee conjuror, an inbred human trait that anthropologists are fond of referring to as "adaptive capacity." The degree of this syncretism can be illustrated by the following anecdote from my father's field notes:

> On the evening of January 1963, a Cherokee woman suffering from chronic headaches was brought on a cot to the Beaver Church campground for a "Christian" healing service. A medicine man sat at her head while a minister stood at her right and the worshippers collected around her. While the minister silently prayed for his charge, the medicine man arose and led the group in a stirring rendition of "Amazing Grace."

The historical success of this ironic, ideological merger can best be evaluated by examining some of the local folk wisdom that permeates the native communities of northeastern Oklahoma. There, it is commonly held that a conjuror who is not a devout Christian should be viewed with some suspicion because "he'd be too fallen in sin to work up a good spell" (Tse:gi Ganv:hnawó:i field notes n.d.).

Cognitive Approaches

As has been shown, functionalist theories are extremely useful in explaining, from a historical perspective, the upsurge of witch-sorcerer phobias among Cherokees during periods of social unrest. Functionalism, however, is not without its critics. According to its detractors, its main weakness is its "obsessive concern with integration" (Nutini and Roberts 1993, 13). Some anthropologists, notably Kennedy (1969), have chosen to view witchcraft as "an institutionalized system of psychopathology" and have asserted further that "we should seriously entertain the possibility of the existence of 'sick societies' or pathological institutions and cultural patterns, rather than asking the a priori relativistic assumption that all groups automatically find a healthy balanced level of functioning" (Kennedy 1969, 167).

I agree with Kennedy that "witchcraft is primarily a manifestation of strongly held negative emotions" (Kennedy 1967, 223). As such, within a narrow psychiatric framework the whole phenomenon can be viewed as essentially a set of socially sanctioned psychosomatic expressions (cf. Lévi-Strauss [1963] 1967, 36) One risks limiting oneself theoretically and creating an intellectual cul-de-sac, however, by attaching such western value judgments as "dysfunctional" to societies whose supernatural belief systems, appear, from a western clinical perspective, as deviant from one's own.

More recent anthropological studies of witchcraft (Nutini and Roberts 1993) have emphasized an epistemological approach that regards these folk beliefs not as "isolated" or "deviant" but as part of a larger established cognitive system. The prescribed focus here is to illuminate "the epistemic and psychological reality of the consequences of supernatural beliefs in sociophysical settings that are as controllable and circumscribed as one can possibly establish" (Nutini and Roberts 1993, 23).

This epistemological approach relies heavily on the concept of cultural conditioning. Viewed from this perspective, "it follows that all effective witchcraft and sorcery systems are self-fulfilling" because they represent a confirmation of one's worldview (Nutini and Roberts 1993, 14).

This cognitive approach owes a debt to Lévi-Strauss's earlier observations about how the "power of suggestion" works in folk societies. According to Lévi-Strauss, the efficacy of magic in the "shamanistic" complex depends upon the strength of three interrelated psychological factors: "first, the sorcerer's belief in the effectiveness of his techniques; second, the patient or victim's belief in the sorcerer's power; and, finally the faith and expectations of the group"(Lévi-Strauss [1963] 1967, 24).

Both medical anthropologists and psychiatric therapists from the era of Freud and Charcot onward would agree that the common denominator affecting the victim of witchcraft or the patient suffering from phobias involves "the power of suggestion." Many of the healing techniques used in modern therapies center on placebo effects that allow patients to achieve self-autonomous cures either through the act of catharsis, faith in the treatment, the healing relationship, or because patients have been conditioned to view their diseases in a certain positive light (Torrey 1986; Moerman 1979, 1983).

By contrast, the operative principle in witchcraft involves the "nacebo" effect, which seems inextricably linked to patients'/victims' tacit acceptance that paranormal phenomena (witchcraft) could exist within their epistemological schemes. When certain external traumatic conditions occur, individuals become susceptible to this power of suggestion (even if it appears from a western perspective that these human reactions are "irrational").

To explore fully the dynamics of witchcraft and sorcery among the western Cherokee one needs to identify those culturally induced "trigger mechanisms" that arouse strong psychological aversions within this study group. To do this one needs to examine certain Cherokee attitudes toward supernaturalism.

Case 2: Siquinid

Between 1961 and 1966 a vigorous correspondence developed between my late father, a university professor living in Dallas, Texas, and his principal informant, Siquinid, a middle-aged, full- blood Indian Baptist minister of mixed Cherokee and Creek ancestry who lived in the back-woods of northeastern Oklahoma near Welling. As a result, I have in my possession some forty letters written by Siquinid to Tse:gi (my late father), which attest to the close relationship that developed between the anthropologist and his native source.

The format of these letters is somewhat surprising. Both men could read and write in the Sequoyan syllabary, and both were equally fluent in Cherokee. Siquinid, however, who lacked a formal education, insisted upon communicating with my father in English, a language for which he had little aptitude or training. As a result, Siquinid wrote in a curious pidgin English style replete with grammatical errors and unusual sentence constructions. One can only assume that Siquinid labored under the burden of this tricky and uncertain discourse for reasons of personal pride because he was aware that his friend and colleague, Tse:gi, held a higher social status than he.

My father employed Siquinid to travel the backroads of Oklahoma to buy or to barter Cherokee medicomagical texts from his relatives, neighbors, or from various traditionalists who had access to such shamanistic writings. Siquinid seems to have had both monetary and personal motivations for acquiring this esoteric knowledge. When he was not preaching at the local church, Siquinid dabbled in folk medicine himself.

A number of Siquinid's prospects did not possess medicine books, as such, in their homes, but they had a number of formulae memorized, which they were willing, for a price, to divulge to him. A widow, whom Siquinid referred to as a "great witch," offered to teach him what she knew from memory about "conging" and "roots of medicine" and "how to fix tobbacco [sic]." The agreed-upon price for these lessons was $2.50 per formula.

Occasionally, Siquinid would incur the wrath of his own relatives over his book-collecting habit. In a letter dated March 6, 1962, Siquinid writes about a kinsman who was particularly offended by this passing on of Cherokee secrets: "Well, its funny way this Indian feel about it. Well, they said this conging Book is not a play thing. . . . Well this old man . . . he is very Conging man. . . . well this old man is my great old grandpa. . . ."

Besides his interest in medicine books, Siquinid evidently had his sights set on acquiring some ritual paraphernalia that once belonged to his father, a medicine man named "Charley Fierce." These ceremonial objects were stored at the house of his grandfather. When Siquinid broached the subject of removing his father's belongings, his grandfather voiced his strong disapproval: "Well he told me about this outfit is very Danger[ous]. Well he said not to come Back anymore his place." (Siquinid, March 6, 1962).

Undaunted by his grandfather's admonitions about the perilousness of his quest, Siquinid decided in the summer of 1963 to solicit shamanistic knowledge from a Cherokee elder, S. M., who lived near the native community of Rock Fence in southern Sequoyah county. During his first trip to see S. M., Siquinid experienced some unforeseen difficulties: "Well I started to S. M. place. Before got there one my tire Blowout wide open. I just had to come Back home. I dident [sic] get there to S. M. But I sure got Bad happen. that Big Skilly Sure Like got me. . . . Well Tse:gi if you send some more money I am ready to go back up the mountain and Let the Big Hoge [sic] Eat me up.

Although Siquinid characterized S. M. as a "cranky old man" who wanted too much money for his medicine books, he returned to Rock Fence the very next week and reluctantly paid S. M. an exorbitant price for his notebooks because he was "kind been fraid the old man . . . I begin thought he might cong me." Despite this concession Siquinid did not escape further misfortune. Driving back to his Welling home, the spindle bolt broke and his car careened into a highway fence post. Even though he managed to emerge unscathed, later, in a letter written on July 17, Siquinid surmised that his car trouble was the result of supernatural interference: "I think Something wrong with me. I do Belive [sic] Someone must Be doing Some congin me. Just in case you and I had a Bad Luck Every time we go over there to Rock Fence. But this coming Saturday I am going to See the witch man. and get tell me Something if Someone congin us. . . . Before the Big Sour Hog eats us up."

Siquinid does not record whether his visit to "the witchman" was successful or not in relieving his misfortunes brought on by "conjuring." Siquinid never stated, for the record, whether he believed his troubles stemmed from a personal conflict with the formidable S. M., or with his grandfather or if they were caused by the "Big Sour Hog," Siquinid's code name for any unidentified, malevolent, supernatural force.

From his letters it appears that Siquinid's attitude toward traditional

Cherokee medicine was somewhat ambivalent. During the fall of 1963, however, he fell ill with a heart condition, and in a letter written on October 22 of that year Siquinid attributed his recovery to the miraculous power of native medicine: "I am Bad Sick; that Hart [sic] trouble Sure like got me down under the ground. I thought I was already dead. well doctor dident [sic] do to [sic] good for me. So they went got the Indian doctor. well finley [sic] he doctor me. and I did come Right Back up my Life."

Mindful, however, that witches have the power to circumvent his treatment, Siquinid qualifies his improved condition with this caveat: "I ges [sic] I be all Right pretty soon. I hope. I think that Big Sour Hog looking for me all time." Thus, it appears that Siquinid still harbored suspicions that someone with a grudge (perhaps S. M. or his own grandfather) was the actual source of his health problems.

Both the Siquinid documents and the case history of E. N., offer revealing glimpses into the epistemological system subscribed to by fullblood Cherokees of the last generation. From this cultural frame sudden life changes (e.g., Siquinid's heart trouble and E. N.'s cancer) are perceived as manifestations of supernatural phenomena.

To explore this issue further Arthur Kleinman's theoretical distinction between disease and illness serves as a useful model from which to conduct an analysis. Kleinman defines the term *disease* narrowly as a "malfunctioning of the biological and/or psychological processes," whereas he differentiates illness more broadly as a "psychosocial experience" or as "a reaction to an imagined, perceived, or even desired disease" (Kleinman 1980, 72, 74).

Although disease and illness are often epiphenomenally intertwined, Kleinman suggests a further distinction: "Disease affects single individuals, even when it attacks a population; but illness most often affects others as well (e.g., family, social network, even at times an entire community) (Kleinman 1980, 73). To complicate matters, illness can manifest in the absence of organic disease (e.g., psychiatric disorders) just as a disease can manifest (e.g., massive trauma) in the absence of an "illness experience" (Kleinman 1980, 74).

Both Cherokee and western medicine acknowledge that prolonged psychosocial stress (either acute or chronic) can negatively affect human immune systems and can produce psychological or physiological impairment in individuals (cf. McElroy and Townsend 1979). These two traditions differ in the categorization of disease (e.g., among the Pima Indians sorcery is not classified as a "real" sickness [Bahr et al. 1974, 19]) and, of course, in the treatment of the resulting illness.

What interests us here is: why did these two Cherokee individuals, placed in a disruptive, stressful environment, respond in the way that they did? To answer this, we have to consider the interrelationship between environmental stresses and folk symptomatology. According to Selye, a pioneering authority on stress, human responses to environmental stress are "marked by non-specificity. . . . In psychosomatic research, this is known as the problem of 'organ choice', and many theories have been put forward to explain why one organ is 'chosen' and not another" (Helman 1990, 251).

A review of the literature on "conjuring" symptoms experienced by Native Americans reveals a wide range of "organ choice." Among the western Apache Basso notes that paralysis of the limbs or acute pain in various parts of the body and dizziness and general faintness are indicative of "sorcerer's sickness" (Basso 1969, 38). Unmistakable symptoms of witchcraft among the Commanche folk healers of Oklahoma are "spasms and contraction of the arms and hands" (McElroy and Townsend 1979, 294). Madsen enumerates a wide range of witchcraft symptoms among the Nahua-speaking Mestizo populations in central Mexico: insanity, mental retardation, St. Vitus' dance, vomiting, diarrhea, headaches, severe stomach cramps, and miscarriages (Madsen 1989, 232).

As discussed in chapter 1, the classic manifestations of Cherokee conjuring are "vague pains somewhere" (see text 12), and excessive melancholia or *uhĭ:soʔdĭ* ('the blue') (see text 15). These ethnospecific manifestations clearly form part of a culture-bound syndrome much like the phenomenon of Navajo hand trembling (Levy, Neutra, and Barker 1989), the outbreak of *"Wihtigo"* among the Cree, Ojibway, and Salteaux (Lehmann 1975), or the bouts of magical fright suffered by victims of voodoo (Cannon [1942] 1972).

Case 3: Sadie

In a third case, a full-blood Cherokee attributed her unusual health condition to being "conjured." "Sadie," a female in her thirties, was treated for an extreme case of dermatitis at a local government hospital in Stilwell, Oklahoma, during the winter of 1965. The attending white physician, baffled by the extreme inflammation of the patient's skin, sent Sadie to Oklahoma City University Hospital and to a clinic in Ft. Smith, Arkansas, for further diagnostic tests.

The laboratory tests were inconclusive, but based on the extremeness of the patient's symptoms, a preliminary diagnosis was advanced of Hansen's Disease (a form of leprosy). Sadie told an interviewer that she had been conjured by a medicine man whom she had offended (Tse:gi Ganv:hnawó:i field notes n.d.).

I do not have access to the full case history of this patient. Western clinical psychologists might suggest, however, that in such cases of probable psychosomatic origin the "severity of the symptoms is usually related to an emotional disorder such as sexual conflicts or lack of self-esteem (Wolman 1988, 148).

Cancer, heart problems, or dermatitis are not medical conditions that the average Cherokee traditionalist would normally attribute to the effects of witchcraft or sorcery. Upon reflection, what seems to have triggered the hysterical response in all three of these individuals was the perceived suddenness of the trauma. The facts surrounding the case of Sadie are incomplete. Siquinid's heart condition, however, was unexpected. Even more remarkable is the case of E. N., for during the 1970s, according to Indian health statistics, Oklahoma Cherokees exhibited an extremely low incidence of cancer (known in Cherokee as *adayé:sgi* ['eater']) in any form. During this period the contraction of a rare and deadly disease such as multiple myeloma, especially among Native American populations, would be considered an extremely unlikely possibility.

Another striking aspect of the three cases is the physical severity of the conditions. Sadie was literally hospitalized by her dermatitis outbreak, Siquinid nearly expired from his attack, whereas E. N. lived less than one year after her initial diagnosis after suffering from extreme bone pain, loss of weight, and spontaneous fractures.

One can put this hysterical reaction to supernaturalism into perspective by noting that the highest mortality rates among Oklahoma Cherokees during the 1960s and 1970s were the result of diabetes mellitus (from which Siquinid finally succumbed in 1980) and alcoholism. It is interesting that as devastating as these diseases have been (it was estimated in 1974 that "roughly one-third of Oklahoma full-blood Indians more than thirty years of age" suffered from diabetes [Wiedman 1979, 10]), neither of these deadly disorders is considered by Cherokees to be a by-product of witchcraft or sorcery.

One can conclude that, according to the Cherokee traditional point of view, chronic diseases (e.g., alcoholism, diabetes) that manifest over time cannot properly be regarded as symptomatic of witchcraft. The telling feature of being "conjured" to the Cherokee mind (as it is to the western Apache, cf. Basso 1969, 38) seems to be the suddenness and severity of the outbreak.

Crucial to the dynamics of Cherokee symptomatology is the cultural frame or normative idealogical expectations of the group. As Kleinman has observed, "Culture influences the cognitive appraisal of external stimuli; it helps determine whether they will be evaluated as stressful or not" (Kleinman 1980, 79). By establishing the moral and ethnical standards of a group and by articulating "what constitutes 'success' (as opposed to 'failure'), 'prestige' (as opposed to 'loss of face'), 'good' behavior (as opposed to 'bad'), human communities can actually "increase the number of stressors that the individual is exposed to" (Helman 1990, 256).

Traditionalist Cherokees place great cultural value on controlling one's emotions at all times, particularly by holding back negative feelings in public situations that might "give offense" to another individual. This code of etiquette, which disallows face-to-face conflicts and direct acts of aggression while it stresses the virtues of group harmony, has been observed similarly among Athabaskan speakers (cf. Basso 1990; Carbaugh 1990; Scollon 1990; and Wieder and Pratt 1990).

As a result, traditionalists frown upon Cherokees who boast about their abilities in public (cf. Fogelson 1977, 187–89). It might also be noted that conservative Cherokees often take a dim view toward their kin "showing off" through displays of economic wealth (e.g., new car, new house). As a consequence, Cherokees who are perceived to be "on their way up" are likely to be targets of personal criticism or jealousy.

Because of this perception, community-based Cherokees often seek closure in their personal relationships and in one-to-one exchanges with Cherokees with whom they are not well acquainted. Explanations for sudden mishaps and traumatic reversals of fortune are sought, upon reflection, in interpersonal hostilities with friends, neighbors, or relatives that have been left unresolved.

Benson Saler, in his study of supernaturalism among the Quiché Maya, developed an important distinction between witches and sorcerers that has especial relevance to the present analysis of Cherokee conjuring. Noting that both supernatural entities "single out" specific victims, Saler suggested that "the sorcerer is usually motivated by personal feelings directed against specific individuals" whereas the witch "is animated by a perverse delight in harming or harassing any person of virtue and is thus at war with society at large" (Saler [1964] 1967, 92)

Despite their diverse symptomatology the three cited medical cases share a common theme: all three of the victims felt that they had been "violated" by some outside force. William Gilbert, in his 1943 sociological study, astutely noted how "the motive of theft enters largely into the calculations of the natives in attributing reasons for the activities of witches and wizards. The conjurer and the disease-producer are always hovering around the sick bed in order to add some life to their own span of existence" (Gilbert 1943, 296).

It is noteworthy that among the western Cherokee practitioners of witchcraft and sorcery do not steal "property" or material objects for economic gain. Rather, they focus on taking away an individual's health and happiness as a means of "getting even," of settling a score or re-dressing an imagined wrong. This idea that sorcerers engage in "personal vendettas" (either directly on their own behalf or as agents for some offended party), seems to be the motivating factor in the fears and suspicions expressed by all three of the individuals whose case histories have been presented here.

By reviewing these tragic human dramas I suggest that for researchers to account fully for the range of phobias, hysterias, or psychosomatic disorders that manifest as the result of supernatural beliefs, they must not only identify the "trigger" mechanism (e.g., life crisis) but must also take into account the emotional makeup of the individuals, their ideological commitment to a specific cultural frame, and their perceived exposure to stress in their physical environments. Although I knew Si-quinid well, as a child, I had a long and affectionate relationship with E. N. As a result, I am intimately acquainted with the facts of her case and am in a position to describe not only her emotional state but also those external factors that, no doubt, contributed to her belief that she had been "conjured" to death.

First, the results of her lab tests served as the "trigger" mechanism for E. N.'s heightened psychological state. E. N. reacted to her diagnosis of multiple myeloma with a high level of shock, anxiety, and depression. Her reaction was, of course, typical under such circumstances and very similar to what has been observed in studied groups of cancer patients elsewhere (Massie and Shakin 1993). Her immediate family was also dismayed and experienced significant degrees of emotional distress.

To the patient and her family the sudden outbreak of this monstrous life-threatening disease appeared to come out of nowhere. In reality, however, multiple myeloma, like most other forms of cancer, has a long latency period. In the months before she was diagnosed as terminally ill E. N. complained of flulike symptoms and anemia. Therefore, the malignant metastatic growth must have developed over a number of years.

Regarding her emotional makeup during this period, E. N. was somewhat disillusioned with her marriage to the wealthy white businessman, who turned out to be a chronic alcoholic. A few months before she died E. N. confided to me that she planned to divorce him as soon as she "got better."

One of the tensions in their marriage had been her new husband's attempts to shield her from her Cherokee relations, whom he considered "low class" and "ignorant." He seemed to express the same disapproving attitude toward her native beliefs as well.

It is clear that E. N. began to suffer from "culturogenic" stress during this period. It is not certain when one of her sisters came to her with the warning that E. N. had been "conjured" by her old boyfriend. It must have happened, however, within a month or so after her diagnosis. The fact that her own relatives, against the wishes of her white husband, were urging E.N. to seek traditional healing from a *dida:hnvwi:sgi* rather than from a modern cancer facility, must have weighed heavily upon her emotions.

As her condition worsened, E. N. had to be hospitalized, creating an additional burden of environmental stress. Contrary to western notions of hospitals as hygenic and antiseptically clean facilities, traditional Cherokees view hospitals with a certain measure of contempt and alarm. The main concern is that hospitals are "dangerous places," which are from a Cherokee perspective "ritually impure." Whereas western doctors may scrub themselves with soap after treating patients, Cherokee medicine men observe a strict regime of purification rites either by inducing vomiting or by spiritually renewing a text at a flowing stream of water after each encounter with a patient.

Because of this atmosphere of spiritual contamination, hospitals are viewed not as quiet, peaceful places of physical recuperation but as violent metaphysical zones where witches and conjurors are free to roam about molesting patients. From the perspective of a Cherokee traditionalist western doctors have limited diagnostic abilities; they may be able to set a bone, but even the most highly trained physician is powerless to deal with the supernatural.

In the last month or so of her life E. N. was often in a hallucinatory state brought on by infusions of pain-killing drugs. States of altered consciousness are frequently cited as preludes to witnessing paranormal phenomena. E. N.'s vision of the mysterious figure of "Walker" sitting on the edge of her hospital bed was, for her, sine qua non proof that her cancer had been manufactured not by natural causes but by the machinations of a conjuror.

Even though more plausible explanations existed, E. N. maintained until her last breath an unshakeable faith that her life had been put into jeopardy by a jealous ex-boyfriend who had hired a paid supernatural assassin. Regardless of how one views the credibility of E. N.'s belief structure, there is a clear functionalist aspect to her behavior. One sees a "coping" strategy here as the terminally ill individual, faced with an overwhelming loss of personal control, seeks a way not just to "give up" but to assign a rational meaning to her death.

Torn between two conflicting ideological worlds, physically weak, and emotionally drained by guilt and anxiety over her marriage, E. N. sought an explanation for the tragic events of her life and found it in her childhood beliefs. Multiple myeloma was, after all, a rare pathological condition, difficult for even the doctors to understand. Faced with the choice of believing that she was being "murdered" by either a natural disease of unknown origin (cancer), or a supernatural agent of known origin ("Walker"), E. N. chose to believe in the latter, for only a terrifying supernatural specter, an uncontrollable demonic force could have stolen away her life-force so wantonly.

Conclusion

My chief interest in presenting these three case histories has been to focus on the patients' interpretations (or projections) of the causes of their various maladies. It is extraordinary that given a range of explanatory choices these Cherokee patients opted to eschew western biomedical theories of germs and viruses and, instead, preferred to view their psychosomatic symptoms or pathogenic disorders as irrefutable evidence that they were hapless victims of otherworldly persecution.

Viewed from a strictly Freudian perspective, these three individuals could be diagnosed as suffering from *conversion hysteria* (an outmoded and controversial term in modern psychoanalytic thinking largely because its nosology is thought to suffer from "a blizzard of symptoms" [Shorter 1986, 550; cf. Slater 1982]). Despite my reservations about using this much maligned term, the salient feature of classic Freudian conversion hysteria is that the patient's symptoms are thought to reflect "a symbolic elaboration of inner conflict" (Evans 1991, 118). Significantly, all three of these full-blood Cherokees traced their present situations to some past incident involving an unresolved interpersonal relationship.

Finally, one can deduce from these multiple and competing symptomatic explanations that these Cherokee individuals were not "passive recipients of their cultural tradition but should be viewed as "intentional actors actively and creatively engaged in the construction of meaning" (Hollan 1994, 74). Cherokee supernaturalism might best be understood as a mutable and dynamic sociopsychological process that operates within a relatively stable and well-defined ideological base. As a result, even though over the last few years there has been a noticeable deterioration of faith in the existence of witches and sorcerers in northeastern Oklahoma, nevertheless, some facets of these ancient beliefs remain intact, impervious to the modern pressures of acculturation, immune to extinction from science.

From a largely empiricist paradigm under certain conditions some full-blood Cherokees exhibit a set of emotions that might be termed a "belief" in witchcraft and conjuring. From a classic western scientific mold I have postulated that Cherokee witchcraft and sorcery can be explained, at least in anthropological terms, as a "culturally induced form of hysteria, triggered by exacerbating life episodes which create acute stress in an individual."

Cross-cultural studies of illnesses, however, no matter how objectively conducted, are always initiated from some external referent, some cultural frame. To varying degrees scientific investigators labor under the same handicap, namely, that "it is difficult to avoid a strong conviction that our own system of knowledge reflects the natural order" (Good 1994, 3).

Thus, I am certain that Siquinid and the other Cherokee traditionalists of my youth would disagree with my rather narrow assessment. They would probably charge that it is a typical "non-Indian" psychological explanation of what is, to them, essentially a metaphysical problem. In one sense they may be correct that supernaturalism falls more appropriately within the domain of the philosopher and the theologian than that of the social scientist, for much anthropological research centers on the social consequences of folk beliefs rather than judges their intrinsic validity.

It is clear from the documents presented here that during the 1960s and 1970s a number of western Cherokees regarded witchcraft as a "real" and problematic phenomenon. The intensity of this belief can be compared to the current view of AIDS in a 1990s world as a "real" and life-threatening disorder.

Ultimately, witches are "real" to the Cherokee mind because they remain within the realm of possibility. After all, there is a vast literature on the subject: the white man's Bible, the stories told by the elders, and the *idi:gawé:sdi*, the sacred formulae recorded by folk healers for one hundred and fifty years. The average traditionalist would ask, Why would Indian people continue to talk about such things if they were not "real"? Not only this, but there are tantalizing circumstances in one's own life when sudden, unexplainable reversals of fortune or bouts of illness could be ascribed, in a certain light, to the workings of supernatural powers.

From the standpoint of vital statistics one can assert that there is a declining trajectory of full-blood conservative Indians living in northeastern Oklahoma. It is, however, too intellectually precarious to estimate how many modern Cherokees continue to "believe" in the existence of witches and conjurors, especially given the limitations of the databank: a body of transcribed magical texts, a few personal narratives, and a smattering of ethnohistorical accounts.

Of course, in estimating such a thing one would have to qualify the standards of measurement. Are such "irrational beliefs" to be interpreted as literal or as symbolic? In the book, *Belief, Language, and Experience*, Rodney Needham argues that the term *belief* may not really be operative "in the ethnopsychological language of many societies" (Good 1994, 14).

In regard to the ultimate survival of Cherokee supernaturalism, it may be too superficial and ethnocentric to suggest that witches and sorcerers flourish best in the recesses of the human imagination where they serve as enduring and vivid metaphors of the threatening unknown. What one can more easily predict is that traditionalist Cherokees will continue to behave in accordance with their views of the sacred world, a realm where only ancient powers can purify and protect the human spirit from the dark, unseen forces that diminish us all.

Bibliography
Index

Bibliography

Unpublished Sources

Cherokee-English Dictionary. Jack F. Kilpatrick and Anna G. Kilpatrick. Ms. in the private library of the author.

Ganv:hnawó:i, Tse:gi Anthropological Field notes. Ms. in the private library of the author.

Kilpatrick, Alan. "Cherokee War Charms." Ms. in the private library of the author.

Kilpatrick, Jack F., and Anna G. Kilpatrick. "Eastern Cherokee Ethnobotany Reconstructed from the Fieldnotes of Frans Olbrechts." Ms. in the private library of the author.

Sa:wali, Uwe:da:sadhi Collection. Cherokee Magical Formulae Written in the Sequoyah Syllabary. 1865–1965. Ms. in the Western Americana Section, Bienecke Rare Book and Manuscript Library, Yale Univ.

Siquinid correspondence. 1961–1966. Ms. in the private library of the author.

Speck, Frank G., papers. "Medicinal Charms and Conjuring Formulae from Allen Long." Collected by Frank Speck. Ms. in the American Philosophical Library, Philadelphia.

Thomas, Robert K. 1958. "Cherokee Values and World View." Ms. in Univ. of North Carolina Library.

Personal Correspondence. 1974. Ms. in the private library of the author.

Toyanisi, Dlanus, Document. Ms. in the private library of the author.

Published Sources

Adair, James. [1775] 1930. *Adair's History of the American Indians*. Edited by Samuel Cole Williams. Reprint. Johnson City, Tenn.: Watauga Press.

Alcorn, Janis. 1984. *Huastec Mayan Ethnobotany*. Austin: Univ. of Texas Press.

Alexander, J. T., ed. 1971. *A Dictionary of the Cherokee Indian Language*. Compiled by Levi Gritts. Tahlequah, Okla. n.p.

Aquirre Beltran, Gonzalo. 1963. *Medicina y mágica: El proceso de aculturación en la estructa colonial*. Mexico City: Instituto Nacional Indigenista.

Bahr, Donald, Juan Gregorio, David I. Lopez, and Albert Alvarez. 1974. *Piman Shamanism and Staying Sickness*. Tucson: Univ. of Arizona Press.

Basso, Keith H. 1969. *Western Apache Witchcraft*. Tucson: Univ. of Arizona Press.

————. 1990. "To Give Up on Words: Silence in Western Apache Culture." 1990. In *Cultural Communication and Intercultural Contact*, edited by Donal Carbaugh, 303–20. Hillsdale, N.J.: Lawrence Erlbaum Associates.

Boyle, David. [1898] 1986. "The Pagan Iroquois." In *An Iroquois Source Book*, vol. 2, edited by Elisabeth Tooker, 54–196. Reprint. New York: Garland Publishing.

Callender, Charles. 1978. "Illinois." In *Handbook of North American Indians*, edited by Bruce G. Trigger, 673–80 Vol. 15. Washington, D.C.: Smithsonian Institution Press.

Cannon, William. [1942] 1972. "Voodoo Death." In *Reader in Comparative Religion*, edited by William A. Lessa and Evon Z. Vogt, 321–27. 3d ed. Reprint. New York: Harper and Row.

Carbaugh, Donna. 1990. "Intercultural Communication." In *Cultural Communication and Intercultural Contact*, 151–75. Hillsdale, N.J.: Lawrence Erlbaum Associates.

Chafe, Wallace L. 1963. *Handbook of the Seneca Language*. New York State Museum and Science Service, no. 388. Albany.

Chaika, Elaine. 1994. *Language: The Social Mirror*. 3d ed. Boston: Heinle and Heinle Publishers.

Champagne, Duane. 1992. *Social Order and Political Change: Constitutional Governments among the Cherokee, the Choctaw, the Chickasaw, and the Creek*. Stanford, Calif.: Stanford Univ. Press.

Clements, Forest E. 1932. "Primitive Concepts of Disease." Univ. of California Publications in American Archaeology and Ethnology, vol. 2, no. 2. Berkeley and Los Angeles: Univ. of California.

De Baillou, Clemens. 1961. "Contribution to the Mythology and Conceptual World of the Cherokee." *Ethnohistory* 8, no. 1:93–102.

DeMallie, Raymond, Elaine Jahner, and James Walker. 1980. *Lakota Rituals and Beliefs*. Lincoln: Univ. of Nebraska Press.

Douglas, Mary. 1966. *Purity and Danger*. London: Routledge and Kegan Paul.

Duran, Fray Diego. [1579] 1971. *Historia de las Indias de Nueva España e Islas de Tierra Firme*. Translated by Doris Heyden and Fernando Horcasitas. Norman: Univ. of Oklahoma Press.

Eliade, Mircea. 1964. *Shamanism: Archaic Techniques of Ecstacy*. Bollingen Series, no. 76. Princeton, N.J.: Princeton Univ. Press.

Ellis, Florence H. 1989. "Southwest Pueblo." In *Witchcraft and Sorcery of the American Native Peoples*, edited by Deward E. Walker. pps. 191–222 Moscow: Univ. of Idaho Press.

Erickson, Vincent O. 1978. "Maliseet-Passaquoddy." In *Handbook of North*

American Indians. Edited by Bruce G. Trigger, 123–36. Vol. 15. Washington, D.C.: Smithsonian Institution Press.

Evans, Martha Noel. 1991. *Fits and Starts: A Genealogy of Hysteria in Modern France*. Ithaca, N.Y.: Cornell Univ. Press.

Evans-Pritchard, E. E. [1937] 1976. *Witchcraft, Oracles, and Magic among the Azande*. Abr. ed. Oxford: Clarendon Press.

Feeling, Durbin, and William Pulte, eds. 1975. *Cherokee-English Dictionary*. Tahlequah: Cherokee Nation of Oklahoma.

Fenton, William N. [1942] 1986. "Songs from the Iroquois Longhouse." In *An Iroquois Source Book*. Vol. 3, edited by Elisabeth Tooker, 1–34. Reprint. New York: Garland Publishing.

Finkler, Kaja. 1983. "Studying Outcomes of Mexican Spiritualist Therapy." In *The Anthropology of Medicine*, edited by Lola Romanucci Ross, Daniel E. Moerman, and Laurence R. Tancredi, 81–102 New York: Praeger.

Fogelson, Raymond D. 1971. "The Cherokee Ballgame Cycle: An Ethnographer's View." *Ethnomusicology* 15, no. 3:327–38.

———. 1975. "An Analysis of Cherokee Sorcery and Witchcraft." In *Four Centuries of Southern Indians*, edited by Charles Hudson, 113–31. Athens: Univ. of Georgia Press.

———. 1977. "Cherokee Notions of Power." In *The Anthropology of Power*, edited by Raymond D. Fogelson and Richard N. Adams, 185–94. New York: Academic Press.

———. 1979. "Person, Self, and Identity: Some Anthropological Retrospects, Circumspects, and Prospects." In *Psychosocial Theories of the Self*, edited by Benjamin Lee, 67–109. New York: Plenum Press.

Fradkin, Arlene. 1990. *Cherokee Folk Zoology: The Animal World of a Native American People, 1700–1838*. New York: Garland Publishing.

Frazer, James. [1890] 1959. *The Golden Bough*, edited by Theodor H. Gaster. Abr. version. New York: New American Library.

———. [1933] 1966. *The Fear of the Dead in Primitive Religion*. Reprint. New York: Biblo and Tannen.

Gearing, Fred. 1962. "Priest and Warriors: Social Structures for Cherokee Politics in the 18th Century." Memoir 93, American Anthropological Association, vol. 64, no. 5, pt. 2.

Gilbert, William Harlan, Jr. 1943. "The Eastern Cherokee." Bureau of American Ethnology Bulletin 133, Anthropological Papers, 23:169–413, Washington, D.C.: Smithsonian Institution.

Gimbutas, Marija. 1989. *The Language of the Goddess*. New York: Harper and Row.

Gingerich, Willard. 1987. "Heidegger and the Aztecs: The Poetics of Knowing in Pre-Hispanic Nahuatl Poetry." In *Recovering the Word*, edited by Brian Swann and Arthur Krupat. Berkeley and Los Angeles: Univ. of California Press.

Good, Byron J. 1994. *Medicine, Rationality, and Experience*. Cambridge: Cambridge Univ. Press.

Griffith, Francis Llewellyn. 1904–9. *The Demotic Magical Papyrus of London and Leiden*. 3 vols. London: Grevel.

Grinnell, George Bird. 1923. *The Cheyenne Indians*. New Haven, Conn.: Yale Univ. Press.

Helman, Cecil G. 1990. *Culture, Health, and Illness*. London: Wright.

Herrick, James W. 1983. "The Symbolic Roots of Three Potent Iroquois Medicinal Plants." In *The Anthropology of Medicine*. edited by Lola Romanucci-Ross, Daniel E. Moerman, and Laurence R. Tancredi, 134–55. New York: Praeger.

Hoebel, E. Adamson. 1960. *The Cheyennes: Indians of the Great Plains*. New York: Holt, Rinehart, and Winston.

Hollan, Doug. 1994. "Suffering and the Work of Culture: A Case of Magical Poisoning in Toraja." *American Ethnologist* 2, no. 1:74–87.

Holzinger, Charles. 1961. "Some Observations on the Persistence of Aboriginal Cherokee Personality Traits." In *Symposium on Cherokee and Iroquois Culture*, edited by William N. Fenton and John Gulick, 229–37. Bureau of American Ethnology Bulletin 180, Washington, D.C.: Smithsonian Institution.

Howard, James H., and Willie Lena. 1984. *Oklahoma Seminoles: Medicine, Magic, and Religion*. Norman: Univ. of Oklahoma.

Hudson, Charles. 1976. *The Southeastern Indians*. Knoxville: Univ. of Tennessee Press.

Hultkrantz, Ake. 1981. *Belief and Worship in Native North America*, edited by Christopher Vecsey. Syracuse, N.Y.: Syracuse Univ. Press.

James the First. [1597] 1966. *Daemonologie*. Facsimile reprint. New York: Barnes and Noble.

Kan, Sergei. 1989. *Symbolic Immortality: The Tlingit Potlatch of the Nineteenth Century*. Washington, D.C.: Smithsonian Institution Press.

Kennedy, John G. 1967. "Psychological and Social Explanations of Witchcraft." *MAN* 2:216–25.

———. 1969. "Psychosocial Dynamics of Witchcraft Systems." *International Journal of Social Psychiatry* 15, no. 3:165–78.

Kiev, Ari. 1968. *Curanderismo: Mexican-American Folk Psychiatry*. New York: Free Press.

Kilpatrick, Alan. 1991. "Going To The Water: A Structural Analysis of Cherokee Purification Rituals." *American Indian Culture and Research Journal* 4, no. 15:49–58.

Kilpatrick, Jack F. 1967. "The Buckskin Curtain." *Southwest Review* 52, no. 1:83–87.

Kilpatrick Jack F., and Anna G. Kilpatrick. 1964. *Friends of Thunder: Folktales of the Oklahoma Cherokee*. Dallas, Tex.: Southern Methodist Univ. Press.

―――. 1965. *Walk into Your Soul: Love Incantations of the Oklahoma Cherokees.* Dallas, Tex.: Southern Methodist Univ. Press.

―――. 1967a. "Muskogean Charm Songs among the Oklahoma Cherokees." Smithsonian Contributions to Anthropology, vol. 2, no. 3. Washington, D.C.: Smithsonian Institution Press.

―――. 1967b. *Run Toward the Nightland: Magic of the Oklahoma Cherokees.* Dallas, Tex.: Southern Methodist Univ. Press.

―――. 1968. *New Echota Letters: Contributions of Samuel A. Worchester to the Cherokee Phoenix.* Dallas, Tex.: Southern Methodist Univ. Press.

―――. 1970. *Notebook of a Cherokee Shaman.* Smithsonian Contributions to Anthropology, vol. 2, no. 6, Washington D.C.: Smithsonian Institution Press.

Kleinman, Arthur. 1980. *Patients and Healers in the Context of Culture.* Berkeley and Los Angeles: Univ. of California Press.

Kluckhohn, Clyde. 1944. *Navajo Witchcraft.* Boston: Beacon Press.

Lehman, H. E. 1975. "Unusual Psychiatric Disorders and Atypical Psychoses." In *Comprehensive Textbook of Psychiatry,* edited by A. Freedman, H. I. Kaplin, and B. J. Sadock, 1150–61. 2d ed. Baltimore, Md.: Williams and Wilkins.

Lévi-Strauss, Claude. [1963] 1967. "The Sorcerer and His Magic." In *Magic, Witchcraft, and Curing,* edited by John Middleton, 23–41. New York: Natural History Press.

Levy, Jerrold E., Raymond Neutra, and Dennis Barker. 1989. *Hand Trembling, Frenzy Witchcraft, and Moth Madness.* Tucson: Univ. of Arizona Press.

Lewis, I. M. 1971. *Ecstatic Religion.* Harmondsworth, Eng.: Penguin Books.

Lopez Austin, A. 1988. *Human Body and Ideology.* Translated by T. Ortiz de Montellano and B. R. Ortiz de Montellano. 2 vols. Salt Lake City: Univ. of Utah Press.

Lounsbury, Floyd G. 1961. "Iroquois-Cherokee Linguistic Relations." In *Symposium on Cherokee and Iroquois Culture,* edited by William N. Fenton and John Gulick, 11–23. Bureau of American Ethnology Bulletin 180. Washington, D.C.: Smithsonian Institution.

McCoy, Isaac. [1840] 1970. *History of Baptist Indian Missions.* Reprint. New York: Johnson Reprint.

McElroy, Ann, and Patricia K. Townsend. 1979. *Medical Anthropology in an Ecological Perspective.* North Scituate, Mass.: Duxbury Press.

McLoughlin, William G. 1984. *Cherokees and Missionaries 1789–1839.* New Haven, Conn.: Yale Univ. Press.

―――. *Cherokee Renascence in the New Republic.* 1986. Princeton, N.J.: Princeton Univ. Press.

―――. 1994. *The Cherokees and Christianity, 1794–1870.* Athens: Univ. of Georgia Press.

Madsen, William. 1989. "Mexico: Tecospa and Tepepan." In *Witchcraft and Sorcery of the American Native Peoples*, edited by Deward E. Walker, Jr., 223–43 Moscow: Univ. of Idaho Press.

Mair, Lucy. 1969. *Witchcraft*. New York: McGraw-Hill.

Massie, Mary Jane, and Elisabeth J. Shakin. 1993. "Management of Depression and Anxiety in Cancer Patients." In *Psychiatric Aspects of Symptom Management in Cancer Patients*, edited by William Breitbart and Jimmie C. Holland, 1–21. Washington, D.C.: American Psychiatric Press.

Middleton, John. 1963. "Witchcraft and Sorcery in Lugbara." In *Witchcraft and Sorcery in East Africa*, edited by John Middleton and E. H. Winter, 257–75. New York: Praeger.

Mihesuah, Devon A. 1993. *Cultivating the Rosebuds: The Education of Women at the Cherokee Female Seminary 1851–1909*. Urbana: Univ. of Illinois Press.

Miller, Jay. 1994. "The 1806 Purge among the Indiana Delaware: Sorcery, Gender, Boundaries, and Legitimacy." *Ethnohistory* 41, no. 2:245–66.

Moerman, Daniel E. 1979. "Anthropology of Symbolic Healing." *Current Anthropology* 20, no. 1:59–80.

———. 1983. "Physiology and Symbols: The Anthropological Implications of the Placebo Effect." In *The Anthropology of Medicine*, edited by Lola Romanucci-Ross, Daniel E. Moerman, and Laurence R. Tancredi, 156–67. New York: Praeger.

Mooney, James. 1891. The Sacred Formulas of the Cherokees. Seventh Annual Report of the Bureau of Ethnology, 1885–1886. Washington, D.C.: Bureau of American Ethnology.

———. 1900. "Myths of the Cherokee." Nineteenth Annual Report of the Bureau of American Ethnology, pt. 1. Washington, D.C.: Bureau of American Ethnology.

Mooney, James, and Frans Olbrechts. 1932. "The Swimmer Manuscript." Bureau of American Ethnology Bulletin 99. Washington, D.C.: Smithsonian Institution.

Morgan, Henry. [1851] 1972. "The League of the Ho-Do-No-Sau-Nee or Iroquois." Reprint. New York: Corinth Books.

Morris, Brian. 1987. *Anthropological Studies of Religion*. Cambridge: Cambridge Univ. Press.

Nutini, Hugo G., and John M. Roberts. 1993. *Bloodsucking Witchcraft*. Tucson: Univ. of Arizona Press.

Olbrechts, Frans. 1930. "Some Cherokee Methods of Divination." *Twenty-third Proceedings of the International Congress of Americanists*, 547–552. New York: Science Press Printing Co.

Ortiz de Montellano, Bernard R. 1990. *Aztec Medicine, Health, and Nutrition*. New Brunswick, N.J.: Rutgers Univ. Press.

Park, George K. [1963] 1972. "Divination and Its Social Contexts." In *Reader in Comparative Religion*, edited by William A. Lessa and Evon Z. Vogt, 381–92. New York: Harper and Row.

Parker, Willard Z. 1938. *Shamanism in Western North America*. Evanston, Ill.: Northwestern Univ.

Parsons, Ellie Clew. 1939. *Pueblo Indian Religion*. Vols. 1 and 2. Chicago: Univ. of Chicago Press.

Perdue, Theda, ed. 1983. *Cherokee Editor: The Writings of Elias Boudinot*. Knoxville: Univ. of Tennessee Press.

Powers, William. 1986. *Sacred Language: The Nature of Supernatural Discourse in Lakota*. Norman: Univ. of Oklahoma Press.

Reid, John Phillip. 1970. *A Law of Blood: The Primitive Law of the Cherokee Nation*. New York: New York Univ. Press.

Reyburn, William D. 1953. "Cherokee Verb Morphology I." *International Journal of American Linguistics* 19:172–80.

Rubel, Arthur J., Carl W. O'Nell, and Rolando Collado-Ardon. 1984. *Susto, A Folk Illness*. Berkeley and Los Angeles: Univ. of California Press.

Ruiz de Alarcon, Hernando. [1629] 1982. *Aztec Sorcerers in Seventeenth Century Mexico: The Treatise on Superstititions*. Translated and edited by Michael D. Coe and Gordon Whittaker. Institute of Mesoamerican Studies Publication no. 7. Albany: State Univ. of New York.

Sahagun, Fray Bernardo de. [1577] 1950–69. *Florentine Codex: A General History of the Things of New Spain*. Translated and edited by Charles E. Dibble and Arthur J. O. Anderson. 12 vols. Salt Lake City: Univ. of Utah Press.

Saler, Benson. [1964] 1967. "Nagual, Witch, and Sorcerer in a Quiché Village." In *Magic, Witchcraft, and Curing*, edited by John Middleton, 69–99. New York: Natural History Press.

Scancarelli, Janine. 1994. "Another Look at a 'Primitive Language'." *International Journal of American Linguistics* 60, no. 2:149–60.

Scollon, Ronald, and Suzanne Wong-Scollon. 1990. "Athabaskan-English Interethnic Communication." In *Cultural Communication and Intercultural Contact*, edited by Donal Carbaugh, 259–86. Hillsdale, N.J.: Lawrence Erlbaum Associates.

Shimony, Annemarie. 1989. "Eastern Woodlands: Iroquois of Six Nations." In *Witchcraft and Sorcery of the American Indian Peoples*, edited by Deward E. Walker, Jr., 141–65. Moscow: Univ. of Idaho Press.

Shorter, Edward. 1986. "Paralysis: The Rise and Fall of a Hysterical Symptom." *Journal of Social History* (Summer):549–82.

Sigerist, Henry E. 1951. *A History of Medicine: Primitive and Archaic. Medicine.* Vol. 1. Oxford: Oxford Univ. Press.

Simmons, Marc. 1980. *Witchcraft in the Southwest*. Lincoln: Univ. of Nebraska Press.

Simmons, William. 1978. "Narragansett." In *Handbook of North American In-*

dians, edited by Bruce G. Trigger, Vol. 15. 190–97. Washington, D.C.: Smithsonian Institution Press.

Slater, Eliot. [1976] 1982. "What Is Hysteria?" In *Hysteria*, edited by Alex Roy, 37–40. New York: John Wiley and Sons.

Speck, Frank G. 1964. "The Creek Indians of Tsakigi Town." Memoirs of the American Anthropological Association. Vol. 2, pt. 2.

Speck, Frank G., and Leonard Broom. [1951] 1983. *Cherokee Dance and Drama*. Reprint. Norman: Univ. of Oklahoma Press.

Spindler, Louise. 1989. "Great Lakes: Menomini." In *Witchcraft and Sorcery of the American Native Peoples*, edited by Deward E. Walker, Jr., 39–74. Moscow: Univ. of Idaho Press.

Staller, Natasha. 1994. "Babel: Hermetic Languages, Universal Languages, and Anti-Languages in Fin de Siècle Parisian Culture." *Art Bulletin* 76, no. 2:336.

Stevenson, Matilda Coxe. 1915. "The Ethnobotany of the Zuni Indians." Thirtieth Annual Report of the Bureau of American Ethnology, 1908–1909, Washington, D.C.: Bureau of American Ethnology.

Swanton, John R. 1911. "Indian Tribes of the Lower Mississippi." Bureau of American Ethnology Bulletin 43. Washington, D.C.

———. 1928. "Religious Beliefs and Medical Practices of the Creek Indians." Forty-second Annual Report of the Bureau of American Ethnology, 1924–25. Washington, D.C.: Bureau of American Ethnology.

Thwaites, Reuben Gold, ed. 1847. *The Jesuit Relations and Allied Documents: Travels and Explorations of the Jesuit Missionaries in New France 1610–1791*. Cleveland, Ohio: Burrows Brothers.

Torrey, E. Fuller. 1986. *Witchdoctors and Psychiatrists*. New York: Jason Aronson.

Turner, Victor. 1975. *Revelation and Divination in Ndembu Ritual*. Ithaca, N.Y.: Cornell Univ. Press.

Wahrhaftig, Albert L. 1965. "Social and Economic Characteristics of the Cherokee Population of Eastern Oklahoma." Carnegie Cross-Cultural Education Project. Chicago: Univ. of Chicago.

Walker, Deward E., Jr., ed. 1989. *Witchcraft and Sorcery of the American Native Peoples*. Moscow: Univ. of Idaho Press.

Wallace, Anthony F. C. 1972. *The Death and Rebirth of the Seneca*. New York: Vintage Books.

Washburn, Cephas. [1869] 1971. *Reminiscences of the Indians*. New York: Johnson Reprint.

Watanabe, John. 1990. "From Saints to Shibboleths: Images, Structure, and Identity in Maya Religious Syncretism." *American Ethnologist* 17, no. 1:131–50.

Wieder, D. Lawrence, and Steven Pratt. 1990. "On Being a Recognizable Indian among Indians." In *Cultural Communication and Intercultural Contact*, edited by Donal Carbaugh, 45–64. Hillsdale, N.J.: Lawrence Erlbaum Associates.

Wiedman, Dennis William. 1979. "Diabetes Mellitus and Oklahoma Native Americans: A Case Study of Culture Change in Oklahoma Cherokee." Ph.D. diss., Univ. of Oklahoma.

Wilbert, Johannes. 1993. *Mystic Endowment: Religious Ethnography of the Warao Indians*. Cambridge, Mass.: Harvard Univ. Press.

Wilson, John A. 1951. *The Culture of Ancient Egypt*. Chicago: Univ. of Chicago Press.

Wilson, Monica. 1957. *Rituals of Kinship among the Nyakyusa*. London: Oxford Univ. Press.

Witherspoon, Gary. 1977. *Language and Art in the Navajo Universe*. Chicago: Univ. of Chicago Press.

Witthoft, John. 1946. "Bird Lore of the Eastern Cherokees." *Journal of the Washington Academy of Sciences* 36, no. 11:372–84.

———. 1983. "Cherokee Beliefs about Death." *Journal of Cherokee Studies* 8, no. 2:68–72.

Wolman, Benjamin B. 1988. *Psychosomatic Disorders*. New York: Plenum Medical Book.

Woodward, Grace Steele. 1963. *The Cherokees*. Norman: Univ. of Oklahoma Press.

Index

Fenton, William, 37
Finkler, Kaja, 103
Florentine Codex, xiii
Fogelson, Raymond, xv, 6, 10–13, 16
Fradkin, Arlene, 9
Frazer, James, xiii, 21–22, 76
Freud, Sigmund, 133, 142
Friends of Thunder (Kilpatrick and Kilpatrick), xiv
Functionalism, 123–25, 131–32

Ga:dhidv (supernatural missile), 20, 67
Ga:dugi (mutual aid society), 126
"Gambler" (possible term for "conjuror"), 12
Gidhayo:hi ('cherry tree place' dialect), 45
Gilbert, William, 53, 139–40
Grinnell, George, 20
"Going to the Water" (purification rite), xviii, 129; color schemes in, 34; and divining rites, 59–60; general description of, 99–100; protective spells in, 71, 77; ritualisms in, 39, 60; and translations of texts, 104–20
Golden Bough, The (Frazer), xiii, 21

'Harmony' ideal, 126
Hicks, Jane, 127
Hoebel, Adamson E., 20
Howard, James and Willie Lena, 38
Huastec Indians, 102
Huron Indians, 17, 19

Idi:gawé:sdi (medico-magical texts), xiv, xvii, 13, 24–25, 53; actualization of magic in, 29; color schemes in, 34–35; conservative nature of, 27; Creek Indian loanwords in, 42, 54; identity tag in, 29–30; invocation in, 28, 30–31; negative/positive reinforcement in, 28, 33; physical adjunctives in, 28, 35; reference to witches in, 144;

structure of, 28–35; and synthesis, 33; time conflation in, 32–33
Imitative magic, 21–22
Iroquois Indians: culturally bound fears of, 125; divining with "spider roots" by, 62; feasts for the dead of, 76; imitative magic of, 21; paranoid attitude toward witches by, 124; and tea to ward off spirits, 76; witches among, 4; wordplay of, 37
Itsodi:yi ('Echota-place' dialect), 45

James I (king of England), xiii
"Juggler" (term for Indian "conjuror"), 12

Kalona a:ye:li:sgi (Raven Mocker), 9–10
Keetoowah (Night Hawk Society), 13, 41, 130–31
Kennedy, John G., 132
Kilpatrick, Jack F. and Anna G., xiv, 97
Kleinman, Arthur, 136, 139
Kluckhohn, Clyde, xiv, 6. *See also* Functionalism
Kumeyaay Indians, 4

Lakota Sioux Indians, 17
Le Petit, Father, 20
Lévi-Strauss, Claude, 133
Levy-Bruhl, Lucien, 123
Little Men, 15
Long, Allen (relative of Will West Long), 97
Lounsbury, Floyd, xvii

Madsen, William, 137
Magical fright, 137
Mair, Lucy, 11
Maliseat-Passamaquoddy, 17, 102
Melanesia "Ghost Shooters," 19
Menominee Indians: conjurors of, 12; soul loss of, 17; witch dolls of, 21; witches of, 12
Miami Indians, 5